W9-BLO-653

Don't Let My Mama Read This

A SOUTHERN-FRIED MEMOIR

Hadjii

Harlem Moon
Broadway Books
New York

PUBLISHED BY HARLEM MOON

Copyright © 2008 by Hadjii

Published in the United States by Harlem Moon, an
imprint of The Doubleday Broadway Publishing Group,
a division of Random House, Inc., New York.

www.harlemmoon.com

HARLEM MOON, BROADWAY BOOKS, and the HARLEM
MOON logo, depicting a moon and a woman, are trade-
marks of Random House, Inc. The figure in the Harlem
Moon logo is inspired by a graphic design by Aaron
Douglas (1899–1979).

Book design by Nicola Ferguson

Library of Congress Cataloging-in-Publication Data

Hadjii.
    Don't let my mama read this : a southern-fried
memoir / Hadjii. — 1st ed.
       p.   cm.
      1. Hadjii—Childhood and youth. 2. Hadjii—Family.
3. African Americans—Southern States—Biography.
4. African American young men—Southern States—
Biography. 5. African American families—Southern
States. 6. African Americans—Southern States—
Social life and customs. 7. Southern States—Social
life and customs. 8. Southern States—Race relations.
I. Title.

E185.97.H225A3 2008
975'.0496073—dc22
[B]   2007043355

ISBN 978-0-7679-2647-8

PRINTED IN THE UNITED STATES OF AMERICA

10 9 8 7 6 5 4 3 2 1

First Edition

I mean don't get me wrong. I ain't no thug or nothin'. I'm in school and everything, but I ain't no got damn Cosby kid either . . . I got what they call issues . . . And the ladies think that shit is sexy.

Scottie, in the film Somebodies

Contents

Author's Note
No Disclaimers

When I was in college I took an Intro to Acting class, and we would perform various acting exercises, monologues, scenes, what have you. And a lot of times before students got up to perform, they would give a disclaimer or an apology to the class, for whatever reason. Like, "I'm sorry this isn't going to be as good as it's supposed to be because I had to work a double last night so I didn't have enough time to devote the attention to the piece that it deserves." Or, "I get nervous speaking in front of crowds so bear with me." Or, "My father wasn't there for me as a child, therefore you can't possibly expect me to have memorized all of my lines." And all the other dumbass excuses people have for being fuck-ups.

But my instructor was cool. He knew that trick. So he created a law that simply stated, "No disclaimers. No apologies. Apologies are a sign of weakness. Disclaimers just mean that you didn't do what you needed to in order to prepare yourself to get the best outcome. Don't apologize. Get up here, do your scene, and let the chips fall where they may."

And I thought that was a really cool lesson, because he was right. When you think about it, apologies and disclaimers are nothing more than someone's attempt to swing the odds in their favor.

So, that being said, I would like to take a moment to apologize to all of you who are about to read this book, because in all honesty, I don't know what the hell is about to happen.

So I apologize to my dad, because he hated profanity and the *n*-word, and, nigga, I curse throughout this whole fuckin' book. I wish you were here, but your death was probably for the best, because if you were alive you'd kill me after you read this shit, and where would that get us?

I apologize to dumb people because there aren't any pictures in here.

I apologize to the ladies because there aren't any pictures of me in here.

I apologize to my mom and family because even though I'm not really talking about them, everyone will think I am. But hey, can't make an omelet without breaking a few eggs, and if your pain and suffering are going to help me buy a new house, well, then, so be it. Remember, "This is going to hurt me more than it hurts you." Sound familiar?

I apologize to all the people who have played important roles in my life who I failed to mention in the book. It's not that you're insignificant, but since I don't have that great of a vocabulary, for right now we'll just leave it at *insignificant*. But one day I'll buy a thesaurus and find a new word to make you feel better about yourself. Maybe *trivial* will do.

My deepest sympathy goes to the black community because my love of chicken, watermelon, basketball, rap music, broken English, and women of all nationalities is a disgrace to us all. My bad.

I apologize to niggas because I grew up with two loving parents, went to college, never sold crack, haven't been shot, and have good credit. I haven't kept it real worth a damn.

On that note, I owe African Americans an apology because I grew up with two loving parents, went to college, never sold crack, haven't been shot, and have good credit, yet I still have some very niggerish ways about me.

I apologize to white people because "you know how black people do this, and white people do that." I've got a few of those jokes in here. Sorry.

Gay people: yeah, I throw a couple of darts at you, but it's only because I'm inclusive.

I apologize to my publishers because they're cringing at the sight of every word I'm writing.

And I apologize to Bill Cosby. For what? I don't know yet. Just trying to stay ahead of schedule.

I apologize to my girlfriend because of all those times that we've been out at a club or restaurant and some beautiful woman walked in and I began to make fun of her shoes or her big butt or something. That was really just a chance for me to check her out. But let's make one thing clear: if you weren't my woman and I was out with some other girl and you walked into a bar, I'd make fun of you, too, because I think you're gorgeous.

And I send my deepest regrets to all the people who said I would never make it, because I feel like I'm letting you down. Please forgive me for not keeping up my end of the bargain.

To Jesus, God, and the Holy Ghost; I know I've got to repent for this one.

Last but not least, I apologize to all of you who are about to read this book, because some of it's true and some of it's false. Some of it's me and some of it isn't. God forbid, a black man who isn't one-dimensional. Could it be that I'm a storyteller who's just telling stories? The nerve of me.

And to my mama, my family, my church family, my friends, and all the people who've supported me and made this possible, I want to say thank you, because if it weren't for you, there would be no me . . . Or at least that's what they told me to say.

So now, out of respect for your hectic schedules, I'm going to let you go on with your lives, because let's face it: you have a book to read.

Don't Let My
Mama Read This

The Negro
Handbook

Back when I was in college I used to take these creative writing courses, right? And I went to a white
school. I love when white people act like they don't know
what "white school" means. It means a school with a
crappy band.

Anyway, I'd be one of the only black dudes in a class
of about fifteen to twenty-five white people and it never
failed. At the beginning of a new semester we'd get
some assignment asking us to write about our childhood.
"Write what your childhood was like." "How was your

childhood?" "How did you spend your summer?" "Write about Christmas morning." "Write about your family dog." Blah-blah-blah. And then everybody's papers would usually go something like this . . .

As a child I remember lying in my bed with my Raggedy Ann doll until I heard the cockle-doodle-doo of Stanley, the head cock of the farmhouse, which signaled the coming of a new day. The piercing sun would rush through my window as it proceeded to dance across my lily-white forehead. As the soles of my feet would embrace the cold caress of the wooden floor, I'd be greeted by Mr. Whiskers' warm meow. "Meow," Mr. Whiskers would say. Then together Mr. Whiskers and I would embark on our daily journey into the world of the unknown to find out what Mee-Maw [white people call their grandparents all kinds of weird shit] was preparing for our morning dining.

After enjoying the gratifying taste of Idaho's finest cuisine, Mee-Maw, Mr. Whiskers, and I would go out to greet all the animals in the barn. "Hello Mr. Doggie." "Mornin' Mrs. Turtle." "Hola Señor Goat." Then one by one we'd check on all the slaves, I mean helpers. There was Old Man Nate, who'd hum all the latest gospel hymns while farming the land. He'd always say the funniest things about God and how God was preparing a home for him when he died. For some reason it always seemed like Old Man Nate couldn't wait to die, or to go to that "Better Place" where all the black people roamed free, but I knew deep down inside that Old Man Nate was just being silly because let's face it, what could be better than spending your entire life working here on our farm?

Then there was Shirley Williamson, whom we called "Good Girl" for short. Good Girl was an eighty-seven-year-old black woman who still loved nothing better than a hard day's work. I remember sitting in Good Girl's lap as my lips retrieved the salty milk from her sweaty breasts. Then Good Girl would ask me in her sweet and soothing voice reminiscent of the most excellent silk spun by the ever so diligent silkworm. She'd say to me, "Sarah, twelve-year-old girls shouldn't still be suckin' on Good Girl's titties, now should they?—No, don't stop. I was just sayin'."

Then around noon, we'd meet Poopie-Paw (Granddaddy) for lunch. Poopie-Paw and I would hike up the mountain with the basket lunches that Mee-Maw had prepared for us. Once we arrived at our destination we'd sit and eat at a nearby stream. During lunch Poopie-Paw would tell me all these wacky stories about the time Señor Goat kicked Old Man Nate in the shin shattering his leg into several pieces. That's why he decided to go ahead and saw it off. I bet that's one bone Mr. Doggie'll never forget!

And then I'd become depressed because I knew that these days would soon come to an end, for it was the ending of July and the dawning of August. The finale of a great summer in the country and the prelude to another school year in the city. Gone would be the peaceful harmony of congregating birds replaced by the arrival of disagreeing horns arguing in congested traffic. And I would think to myself, "God, thank you for Poopie-Paw, and thank you for Mee-Maw, and most of all God, thank you so much for making me white." Better place for Old Man Nate? Yeah right. What could be better than here on the farm?

Later that night me, Mee-Maw, and Poopie-Paw would feed Good Girl and Old Man Nate. Then we'd say goodnight to all the animals. "Goodnight, Mr. Horsie." "See ya tomorrow, Mrs. Grizzly Bear." "Hasta mañana, Señorita Sheepo." Then Mee-Maw would tuck me in after dinner and gently place her succulent lips on my forehead right after telling me a bedtime tale of how her and Poopie-Paw's great-grandfathers ran all the trespassing Indians off of our land. It was at that point that I realized that I loved my Mee-Maw, and I loved Poopie-Paw, and more than anything, I loved being white.

And everyone would applaud. Then everybody else in the class would read their papers, and everybody thought their childhood was so fuckin' wonderful because theirs were filled with stories of summer cottages, winter cabins, Midwestern farms, California beaches, snowy mountains, foreign countries, and all this other cool shit. It was enough to make you wanna vomit. Because in my mind I would think to myself, "My childhood was pretty cool too. Albeit in its own way." Maybe I ain't have no mountains, but we used to take some bricks and cardboard and make some hellified ramps in the middle of the street and jump'em with our bikes. And maybe we didn't have any streams, but the water hose was a muthafucka in the summertime. What'chall know about playin' in the sprinkler on a hot summer day?

See, there's nothing like growing up black in America. I mean, minus the poverty, unemployment, hate crimes, gang violence, police brutality, racial profiling, and the always present possibility of getting shot in the head over damn near nothing at all, I wouldn't trade it for the world, because growin' up black can be a beautiful thang.

This was until it was time for the other black person in the class to read their paper. That's when it just got fuckin' depressin'. Notice how I say, "The other black person in the class." Because there were always at least two of us. Never more than three, but always at least two. Because at a white school two blacks is enough to make their quota, but four is enough to start a revolution.

And a funny thing happens when there are only two black people in a room full of white folks, because if I'm black and they're black, there's an automatic assumption that we have to get along. It's in the Negro Handbook.

See, there are all types of rules and stuff you've gotta be aware of when you're black, and when we're born the powers that be give us a handbook to make sure we're all on the same page. It gives you all types of important tips and information, like "Race card. Never leave home without it." How to make good potato salad. Jesse Jackson's cellphone number, and a bunch of other vital information that every black person should know.

And it also comes with a set of theories, rules, and procedures. For example, an *n-i-g-g-e-r* is a stupid, ignorant person, but an *n-i-g-g-a* is your friend. Or you could say a *nigga* is a misspelled *nigger*. That's the cool thing about the handbook. Some spots leave room for interpretation. There's also the belief that a black person can never be racist because we don't have the power. Personally, I feel that as an American I have the ability to hate just as good as the next man. How dare you put a limitation on my hate? However, the biggest, biggest rule of them all is that no matter what, whether African American or nigga, male or female, straight, homosexual, rich, poor, or whatever category you fit in, when two black people are in the same room with a bunch of white people, it is mandatory that those two black people take care of one another. This is major! We have to look out for each other. It's in the rules.

For example, if I'm on the bus or the train and it's full, and I see another black person get on and they need a seat, I am by law obligated to scoot over and let them sit down next to me. And if I don't, they can call my ass into headquarters and I'm liable to lose my Negro license. "What'chou in for?" Failure to scoot over. "Nigga what?

You ain't scoot over? That's like on page three. What's the matter wit'chou?"

So anyway, this black dude in class is about to read his paper, right? And I'm thinking, Oh shit. Here we go. Cause he gave me the look. You know, "the look"? The look that somebody gives you to let you know that something's about to happen. The look that says, "I'm about to shake things up, and give'em the real." And I've been around long enough to know that when the other black person in the class gives you the look it usually means that they are about to either (*a*) say what's on their mind, (*b*) tell you how they really feel, (*c*) represent, or (*d*) all of the above. On the other hand, when I give someone my look it means one thing and one thing only, which is, "I don't feel like hearin' that shit today."

The only problem is that most people don't recognize my look. Especially young black men with dreadlocks and nappy beards. You know, one of them niggas that think they're more righteous than you and that you're a sellout because you actually take time out to groom before you walk out of the house, or that a sista ain't keepin' it real because she's got a perm? They think that every black man on the planet should be as black as them. I'm talkin' about if you go to these niggas' houses they've got black fists for doorknobs and shit. I mean these are some real proud of their heritage type cats. And I'm proud of my heritage too. Matter of fact, I'm so proud of it that I don't feel the need to defend it every day, because it's set in stone. I ain't gotta prove nothin' to nobody. It is what it is. But when they shoot me their "I'm about to say what's on my mind" look, and I respond with my "I don't feel like hearin' that shit today" look, they mistake my "I don't feel like hearin' that shit" for "Yeah. Go on 'head and represent, brotha." And off we go with the bullshit.

And usually when the other black person in class feels the need to speak his or her mind on behalf of the race, I don't mind because I know the procedure. No matter how stupid whatever they're about to say may be, all I have to do is nod my head once or twice, giggle when appropriate, and be ready to give the Black Second Opinion, and my job is done. Cause whenever someone's representin', trust me, you're going to have to answer at least one question for confirmation. Example: Someone'll say, "A black man in America can't get no job. Ain't that right, Hadjii?" All I have to do is nod my head, give a little chuckle, and then say, "Preach, nigga." And then I can leave and go to my job.

But to be perfectly honest, it's the first day of a new semester. I don't know anybody. It's nine o'clock in the morning. And personally, I just feel that it's too got damn early in the morning to be representin' already. You ain't even givin' a nigga enough time to get worked up about nothin' yet. My representin' doesn't usually kick in until around twelve-thirty.

Yet today's situation is a little different, because today we're not talking about politics. We're not talking about religion or education. We're not talking about the war. We're talking about childhood. Past experiences.

Relationships. What you've been through. This is personal. So you know what's next? That's right. Here comes the pain.

See, nobody can talk about pain better than black people. I guess it started with gospel music, and the blues, and on and on, but then Tupac came along and took pain to a whole 'nother level. Nobody in the history of entertainment could talk about pain like Tupac could. His pain, your pain, black people's pain, single mother's pain, fatherless children's pain, the hood's pain, the hustler's pain. That's why everybody loved him so much, because he could relate to any and everybody. Pac could write a song about acid indigestion and you felt that shit. If it hurt, he was on top of it. And he lived an interesting life and wasn't afraid to share it with the world, and we loved him for that.

We loved him so much that he inspired us to share our pain and angst about all of the things that we've been going through, so now you've got an entire generation of young people who feel the need to share their personal tragedies and turmoil just like Tupac did. Only problem is, unlike Tupac, the average nigga's life ain't that fuckin' interesting. And unless you can make that shit rhyme over a nice beat, I really don't feel like hearing that shit.

But needless to say, homeboy would go on to read his paper that went something like this:

What was my childhood like? [Insert chuckle.]
You wanna know what *my* childhood was like?
Well, I spent my childhood as a black man. A

young black man in America. I spent my childhood as a suspect. See, all you lily-white, pale-faced, somewhat pinkish undertone lookin' muthafuckas don't even know how good you've got it. On your farms, and in your mansions, and condos with the finest things in life like heat and running water. Cable and silverware, and bowls, and all kinds of other cool shit. You lucky to not have to go through the shit I done been through. You're lucky to not have to live every day of your life lost. Ain't that right, Hadjii?

Umm-hmm. Just the other day I was at the gas station thinking, "Where the fuck am I?" I'm witcha, nigga.

I mean, my mama started out a doctor, my daddy a lawyer. Those are some hard times for a nigga tryin' to find his way. So the only way I could get the things that I needed to survive was to get on the grind and start hustlin'. Know what I'm sayin', Hadjii?

Umm-hmm.

Fuck waitin' 'round on Christmas time or a nigga's birthday. I gotta make a way for me and my family now! I might not even make it to see another Christmas. Seems like everyday, I'm losin' anotha homie to some bullshit. My nigga Big Alex died from leukemia. My homeboy from 'round the way died from pneumonia. All my niggas dying in the streets, in car accidents and shit. It's real out here, but I refuse to drive fifty-five for anybody. I already gotta face the judge in a court of law now 'bout some unpaid parkin' tickets facin' me and I'm just prayin', "Lawd make a way for me nigga cause I'm lost!" Don't you feel that way too, Hadjii?

Umm-hmm.

But it ain't me. The streets made me this way. I know y'all think me and my nigga Hadjii are some crazed animals that need to be in a cage somewhere, but it ain't our fault. It's what society's done to us. The system! My daddy used to leave for work 'round six in the mornin' and sometimes I wouldn't see that nigga again until later that night! And my mama was addicted to cigarettes! Do you know what that does to a kid? Sittin' there watchin' yo mama smoke cigarette after cigarette? Times was hard on a nigga. Besides being on the math team, debate team, drama club, and in the honor society, all a nigga had was the streets. You know what it's like to be in high school and not have enough money to buy your senior pictures? Do ya? You know what that does to your mind? Tell'em what it does to your mind, Hadjii.

Completely fucks it up.

I knew I had to make it happen cause I ain't have no alternative. Either I'ma turn to a life of crime and hustlin' on the streets, or I'ma just sit here and accept this full-paid academic scholarship to Harvard and become a biochemist. No way out, nigga. So I ended up here. Amongst all of you. But I just want you to know one thing. No matter what'chall try to do to me and my nigga Hadjii. No matter how upset you are that we're here. We ain't goin' nowhere! Give us twice the work. Grade us extra hard. Cause we're here and we're here to stay!

Then the professor would say, "Okay, that was interesting. Tell me, Hadjii, what's your life been like?" And I'd be thinkin', "Hmm, I probably could sit here and share a bunch of my personal losses, hard times, embarrassing moments, and stupid decisions wit'chall, but to be perfectly honest, number one, I don't wanna sit around and reminisce about bad times, and number two, that shit ain't really none of your fuckin' business." That's why I refer to it as my "personal" life.

So mine would be something old and something new. Some of it lies, but a lot of it true, and it would usually go something like this:

Crusty Draws, and a
Mother's Pride

Not to be cliché, but for the most part, all black
people, coloreds, Negroes, African Americans, niggas, or
whatever you wanna call 'em this year grow up under
similar circumstances. Not the same, but similar. Because
I couldn't imagine what it would've been like to grow up
in the North in some project building where they've got
everybody stacked forty floors high. Nor can I understand what it must feel like to grow up in a gang-infested
neighborhood where other pressures are forced upon you.
And to be perfectly honest, I can't imagine what it

must be like to grow up in today's times. But even though there are so many differences, so much of it is still the same. For example every neighborhood has the same cast of characters.

First, you've got your Crazy Man—the Crazy Man is usually a black male age thirty-five to sixty-five who has a fondness for wearing either church clothes or biker shorts, MD 20/20, and ten-speed bicycles or grocery buggies and a Walkman, because music is a must-have for crazy people. He can usually be seen pedaling through the streets and getting off of his bike to spew late-breaking news updates he's just received from none other than the Man Upstairs himself since you last saw him, which was only an hour ago. Something like, "God say y'all better get cha soul right because He comin' back down here 'round about four-fifteen! Ain't gonna be no *Monday Night Football* tonight! He also told me to tell one of y'all to run up to the store and bring me back some jellybeans!"

Then there's the neighborhood Nasty Girl. Every neighborhood has the neighborhood Nasty Girl. Unfortunate, but true. This is a girl who's waaaaayyy too sexual at too young an age. This is the girl who's pulling up her shirt for crowds of bystanders, and if you go to her house I guarantee you her daddy's got a not so well-hidden porno collection in the garage or attic or something. Word to the wise: Parents, there is no such thing as a well-hidden porno collection, a hidden gun, a hidden stash of crack, hidden pictures of Mommy naked on your

kid's Big Wheel or any of that shit. If you've got it in your
house, get rid of it now! Cause ya kids are gonna find it.
And not only will they find it, but they're gonna find it
and they're gonna smoke ya crack, have sex with each
other, then shoot each other in the head. Then you're
gonna be on television talkin' about, "How did this happen? I told my kid over and over again, in the event that
you happen to stumble across any of my crack on the coffee table, what's the golden rule? Don't touch it!"

Next if you're lucky you've got the Candy Lady. This
is a woman that's far too old to be exploiting the
sweet tooth of young and unsuspecting children, but she
doesn't care. "I got peppermints for five dollars!" You
greedy thang, you. That's what happens when ya live in a
capitalist society. But I must admit, it's amazing how y'all
get that sugar to stay down at the bottom of that frozen
Kool-Aid icee y'all be pushing. That's a damn good icee.

Then ya got Stacy, Tracy, Shannon, Jeremy, Jamie,
Adrian, Chris, or Tory—every hood had the cool-ass
dude with a two-way name. Like you could name either
a girl or a boy Tory, ya know? More than likely, this
was also the wealthiest cat on the street. Not wealthy
in the sense that he actually had money, but wealthy in
the sense that he was a spoiled muthafucka. Stacy/Tracy/
Shannon/Jeremy/Jamie/Adrian/Chris/Tory were always
"the first ones with shit." You remember when you were
a kid and there were those kids in the neighborhood
or at school who were always the first ones with shit?
They were the first ones to get the new bike, the new bas-

ketball goal, the new trampoline, the new Jordans, the Nintendo, the Starter jacket, the gold chains, the gold tooth, etc., etc. They actually got their clothes off the rack as opposed to the hand-me-downs that the rest of us were used to. They were pretty boys before we even knew what pretty boys were. Imagine P. Diddy now as an eleven-year-old and there you have it. By the way, ain't P. Diddy's first name "Sean," or for the sake of argument "Shaun"? Those dudes with the two-way names are a one-way ticket to success if I've ever seen it! Name a nigga Tyrone and you're just begging for trouble.

And don't forget about Chester Chester the Child Molester. It never fails. There's always that one dude in your neighborhood who likes watching the kids play just a tad bit too much. Usually a middle-aged guy who wears glasses, plaid shorts, with his socks all the way up to his knees, and still lives with his mama. Like everybody'll be at the park playing basketball or something and Chester'll just stand there at the fence for hours. And God forbid one of the kids fell down and scraped their knee or somethin'. Who's the first one there with their portable first-aid kit? Chester! "Oh, lemme see that little fella. Oh, you got a little boo-boo. Lemme blow on that for ya. That feel better? Ya know, you're quite the little athlete. You run so fast. You're a little speed demon, aren't chou? Oooh, I bet you are. I have an Atari in my bedroom. You wanna race me to my house?"

And I could go on and on about the Neighborhood Bully, or the Kid Who's Always on Punishment, the Girly

Boy, or the Crazy Dog that sends fear into the hearts of everybody in the neighborhood whenever he gets loose, but I think you get the point.

We all have somewhat of the same experience. Especially when it comes to ass whuppins. And no, I'm not about to go all over the top with it like they do on TV. "Remember when you was little and yo mama used to beat'cho ass wit' barbwire? She be like, 'Didn't I tell you—!' And yo ass be bleedin' and shit! Then she tie yo ass up and putcha in the bathtub and then throw the radio in that bitch and electrocute yo ass until ya daddy get home! Then once ya daddy get home he pistol-whip yo ass! Y'all remember that?" Nope, sure don't. I guess that was just your abusive past, asshole.

Because, I'm not talkin' about that, but there are a few specific beatdowns that everyone's had. Like there's the "Got Caught in a Lie" beatdown, the "Actin' Up at School" beatdown, the "Grocery Store Parking Lot," the "Caught Playin' with Matches," and my personal favorite, the "Mom/Dad Backseat Reach-Around," to name a few. There's also the ass whuppin in front of ya best friend or cousin who was spending the night. Trust me, nothing can fuck up the fun like gettin' ya ass kicked in front of ya best friend. Vice versa too, cause if your friend gets a beatin' while you're staying at his house, the rest of the evening's shot. However, I'm not talking about any of those instances. I'm talking about one particular beatdown that I got as a child, and I'm sure that a lot of you out there got it too. It goes like this.

Your mom doesn't really care about things like you breaking something, or saying some dumb shit, or farting in public, or any of that. That just means you're normal. Don't get me wrong. She wants you to know the value of stuff and how to appreciate things, but you can still break it and it's no big deal. Like if I broke something in the house, sure my mom would get mad, but she'd get over it. Even if my grades slipped in school a little bit, she would work with me as long as she knew I was doing my best. Whatever that means. But there's one thing that a black woman absolutely, positively will not tolerate in her house. One thing that will send even the most righteous God-fearing woman into a frenzy. And that's them dirty, stinky, nasty, crusty-ass draws! Yeah, I know they're called "drawers," but down south we call them "draws."

Now I don't know what women have got against crusty draws, but trust me, they are enough to drive your mom straight crazy. Most dads think it's funny cause let's face it, theirs ain't much better, but for some reason, moms can't take a joke.

It usually happens around that time when you're like, I guess seven or eight or whatever, and you're still young, but you've gotten too old to still be making those mistakes. Cause women don't look at it like, "Okay, crusty draws? He must've had a bad day today. Maybe he was stressed out?" Nah, women look at it like, "Crusty draws? I'm raising a little nasty bastard! I'm failing as a mother!" Cause women have a lot of pride, and when you're a kid you're unaware of what's going on. It's not until you get older and start dating that you realize that your mom is actually a real woman. I remember times where my mom would be in the kitchen cookin' or somethin' and my dad would walk by and give her a nice little pat on the butt. Nothin' nasty. Just one of them "You still got it baby!" pats, and I'd be thinkin', "What kinda nasty shit is that? Feelin' on my mama. You some kinda pervert or somethin'?"

Cause when you're a kid your mom is, well, Mom. She cooks, cleans, yells, hugs, laughs, dances, protects you from Daddy, reads bedtime stories, cleans up, makes you clean up, goes to the mall, the grocery store, flea market, Salvation Army, church, work, entertains company, irons, blah-blah-blah, and basically loves you to death. That's Mama. She ain't got no feelings. She's too busy doin' motherly shit.

But you know, mamas are cool. They try to talk to you first. They'll come in your room one night and say, "Yo, we need to talk. I think you need to concentrate on wiping your behind a little better after a number two, okay?" and they do their best to keep it real simple and unintimidating, because they've been watchin' *Oprah* and they wanna make sure they don't fuck up ya self-esteem at an early age, because after all, you've got the rest of your life to fuck ya self-esteem up. So they keep it sweet and encouraging like, "Wipe until there's no more brown stuff on the paper. Okay? If you wipe and see brown? Keep wiping. Let's tighten things up around here. I know you can do it."

Then when that approach doesn't work the tone begins to get a little harsher. They call you in the laundry room or take you to the laundry mat with 'em and when they get to your draws they'll be like, "This doesn't even make sense. Look at these! You are too old to be bringin' me draws like this. Get it together." And as a kid, I must say, I hadn't ever seen my mom get too upset before, so when things got to this point, I was like, "Damn. Okay, Mama's startin' to frighten a nigga."

And I tried. I swear I did. I'd wipe and wipe and wipe and pray and pray, check the paper and everything, and later that day while I was tryin' to be productive, my ass would start itching and I'd be like, "Why is my booty itchin'?" And then that night, before I'd take a bath, I'd close my eyes and cross my fingers and pull my draws down, like, "Please God. No crust. No skids." Open my eyes and "Damn! Not again." And I know the clock's ticking by now too, cause now I'm at that stage where I'm spending the night with my cousins and shit like that so now my aunt, who by the way is my mom's sister, has seen my crusty draws too and word of my itchy ass is starting to spread around the family. Now my mom's fed up cause I'm embarrassing her. So one night she kicks in the door to my room and pins me to the bed and puts a pair of my crusty draws to my face and says, "If I find one mo' pair of your underwear lookin' like this, I swear on my life I'ma beat the livin' daylights outta you," and like I said before, I ain't never seen my mom get this mad about anything, so by now, I'm a pretty traumatized cat. So I'm thinkin', "What am I going to do? I tried wiping.

That ain't work. I tried not shittin' at all. Backfired! This woman's gonna kill me if I don't tighten things up. But what can I do? Fuck it. I just ain't eatin' no more."

Well, two hours later, Mom makes spaghetti, and I lose focus. But then I had one of them epiphanies. "I got it!" My dumb ass gets the bright idea that since I fuck up every pair of draws I wear, I'm just gonna wear the same ones over and over. See, my mom did laundry like once a week, so I'ma just wear Sunday's draws all week. Then on Saturday, I'll give her Monday, Tuesday, Wednesday, Thursday, Friday, and Saturday's draws and they all be white as snow (well, I guess they were all off-white by now) and when she sees all them clean draws she's gonna be so proud of me. Hell yeah. I'm a brilliant muthafucka shawty!

So boom. Sunday came. I'm wearin' Sunday's draws. Got off to a rough start too cause by Monday I had already skidded'em up pretty bad, but a plan's a plan. Monday goes by. Tuesday goes by. By Thursday these mufuckas was like pasted to my ass. And my daddy was like, "Damn boy, why all those flies keep followin' you around?" But I'm playin' it cool. Friday goes by. Then came the moment of truth. Saturday.

My mom had a routine. (Note: Everybody has a routine. Fellas, know why so many of us get caught cheating on our girlfriends? It's cause we mess up our routine. Example: Every day you get home from work, you walk inside. Put your bag by the door, look to see what's in the refrigerator, check your messages, turn on the TV, then you change clothes, go to the bathroom, then lay on the couch with your girlfriend or whatever, right? If all the sudden one day, you come home, leave your bag in the car, and then walk inside, she's gotcha. If you change clothes before you check your messages, she's gotcha. Ya can't break ya routine. It's a dead giveaway.) Parents, I don't care how young, dumb, blind, deaf, or whatever your kids are. They've still got your routine down cold. Every Saturday, I'd wake up and watch cartoons until like ten o'clock. Then my mom would get up and throw together a little breakfast. Then while I was eating she'd let me know that it was house cleanin' time. How would she do that? She didn't say it. She didn't make an announcement. It was way more serious than that. She'd go over to the stereo and throw on some Mississippi Mass Choir or Mahalia Jackson. Gospel music. "Oh! We finna clean this house today." Gospel music and cleaning go hand and hand. To this day, no matter where I'm at, every time I hear the Mississippi Mass Choir on the radio I grab a broom and some furniture polish.

Anyway, once breakfast was done and the hymns were on she'd start shaking all that carpet freshener stuff around the house. Every room but the master bedroom cause my daddy would still be in there and he was too manly to be smellin' all that sweet shit. Then after the carpet freshener was down, I'd have to vacuum while she cleaned the bathroom. She never made me clean the bathroom cause she wanted that shit done right. If she can't trust me to keep my own draws clean how's she gonna

trust me with some community shit? Remember, women
have a lot of pride. My mama'll be damned if company
ever popped up on some surprise visit and found us with
a dirty bathroom. Hell nah! Cause again, that doesn't
mean you had a bad day where you didn't get around to
cleaning the bathroom. That meant y'all were some nasty
muthafuckas, and she didn't play that. Cause there ain't
nothin' worse than bein' known as the Dirty House
Family. Cause have you ever met somebody or known
somebody and had a certain level of respect for 'em, but
then you walked into their house and all that admiration
went out the window? I mean you walk into somebody's
house and the roaches were carrying Lysol? Ya ever been
in a house that was so dirty that you put on a condom before you sat on the sofa? That gives you a bad rep. So now
do you see why the crusty draws thing is about to boil
over? My mom's rep is on the line.

So I would vacuum and dust, and she'd do the bathrooms and all the mirrors in the house, cause moms don't
play that streaky-mirror shit neither. By now it would be
like twelve/one o'clock. We both get dressed, cause now
we're about to pick up my grandmama and then go to the
grocery store. They're going to shop. I'm going to play
the video games and read the wrestling magazines. That's
my shit. Remember, I'm like seven years old. After that,
which is damn near like six o'clock in the evening cause
takin' my grandmama grocery shopping was an all-day
ordeal, she'd make you take her forty minutes across
town to use some lame-ass coupon that'll save her thirty

cents on stockings or somethin'. Plus she's still tryin' to look for all these old-ass items from her childhood that modern stores don't sell anymore like lye soap and slaves and shit, but at least she used to buy me them Animal Crackers and canned french fries. It's amazing the nasty crap you can eat when you're a kid. However, I can still get down with a box of Animal Crackers if the mood is right. It's still something very seductive about biting the head off that lion, like, "I'm King Hadjii, you bitch-ass lion!" (Chomp.) But I digress.

So it's six o'clock. We drop Granny off and now we're on our way home. She's thinking about what she has to do for church tomorrow and I'm thinking about my Crusty Draws Cover-Up. We're both on a mission. We walk inside, and like clockwork she barks, "Go getcha dirty clothes." Showtime.

I go in my room and get my dirty clothes bag, which was a cool-ass fishnet bag my dad had brought home from his days in the navy. I kept that bag until like my sophomore or junior year in college and then I lost it. But anyway, I go in my room and grab my bag. By now I had actually changed into another pair of draws and hid my "war draws" behind the dresser. I come out and sit the bag down by the washing machine and everything's smooth as can be, right?

Kids. I don't care how old, dumb, blind, deaf, or whatever you think your mama is, she's got your routine down cold. Usually, after turning my crusty laundry over to my mom, I would take my little humble ass in my room and play with my toys or try to watch *Diff'rent*

Strokes and *The Facts of Life* before I pretended to be reading the Bible. After all, no matter how crusty ya draws are, she can't get too mad at me if I'm readin' the Bible. "Mama, it's too hard to remember to wipe my ass and the Book of Psalms at the same time." But not tonight. Oh, I knew there weren't any skid marks in that bag so you couldn't tell me shit. I'm all up under her like, "Mama, what the fuck is taking you so long? You gonna jump on that laundry or what? By the way, there's this new GI Joe video game a nigga been eyeing for the last few weeks. What'chou gon' do?" Then finally, she washes clothes and goes to bed with no drama. No drama! I stay up and watch some of *Saturday Night Live* with my pops. He'd usually let me watch until they got to the news segment, which was like twelve or twelve-fifteen; and occasionally, once he knew my mom was asleep, he'd let me peek at a booby or two on HBO. Talk about the good life.

I wake up the next morning and her routine's in full swing. My mom would mop every Sunday morning before anybody else got up. Number one, so nobody would walk over her sparkling floor before it dried, and number two, my mom hated—hated—and to this day will still cut'cho ass if you make her late for church. (Even though we were always late for church anyway.) So there was no bullshittin' on Sunday, buddy. Wake up, walk into the kitchen, she'd say, "Eat breakfast, put what'cha wearin' to church on the bed, get in the shower, brush your teeth, and wash your fuckin' face!" (By the way, my mom never cursed or used any profanity toward me a day in her life.

There was no profanity used in our house, yet and still, my parents had a way of saying normal shit that still managed to have a cursing undertone to it. She'd say, "And you better wash your face!" Which to me still sounded like, "Wash your fuckin' face, ya lil' bastard!" But ya know, "tomato-tomahto.") Cause as a kid I was notorious for not washing my face. I always figured, "Fuck it. It's just gonna get dirty again anyway."

So we go to church and we make it through Sunday and we get to Monday, but I notice that my mom keeps looking at me with this strange expression on her face. A look that was like, "I'm gonna get to the bottom of this." And then, Monday night, it happened. My mom came in my room and said—well, lemme give it to you like this.

SCENE: BEDROOM, EARLY EVENING.
I'm in the middle of the floor playing with action figures. Mom enters.
ME: (happy) Hey Mom.
MOM: (not happy) We need to talk.
ME: (innocent) Whatever's the matter, Mother?
MOM: I washed clothes last night and noticed none of your underwear in the dirty clothes.

Then it hits me.

ME: (thinking internally) *Got damn it! I forgot to insert the clean draws into the dirty clothes. I better think of an answer fast.* (aloud) Uhh? What—

MOM: (furious) Don't tell me yo little nasty ass is
   runnin' around here with no draws on!
ME: (appalled) Hell yeah I wear draws. You think I'm
   some kind of freak or somethin'?
MOM: (furious and confused, a bad combination)
   Well then, where the dirty ones at?
ME: (buying time) Uhhh?
MOM: Take me to them now!
ME: (humble) Here they go.

I go and reach down behind the dresser and pull out
a pair of now mahogany brown, cardboard-stiff underwear and hand them over to her.

MOM: (speechless . . . morbid) Where are the rest of
   them?

And it's at that very moment that I begin to realize the
magnitude of my sins, because my sweet mama who
cooks, cleans, yells, hugs, laughs, dances, protects me
from Daddy, reads bedtime stories, cleans up, makes me
clean up, goes to the mall, the grocery store, flea market,
Salvation Army, church, work, entertains company,
irons, blah-blah-blah, and basically loves me to death,
turns her back on me. She can't even look at me. Then
she repeats the question.

MOM: Where are the rest of them?
ME: (just all fucked up) . . . That's it.

MOM: (disappointed, perturbed, livid, perplexed, bewildered, hostile, nauseous, and downright disgusted and pissed off!) What!

ME: See, what had happened was—

MOM: You been wearin' the same draws all week?

ME: Yeah, but—

MOM: So you mean to tell me that after you got outta the tub, you been puttin' the same dirty draws back on?

ME: Well, I ain't never really look at it like that, but I guess when ya put it that way, uhh, yeah?

MOM: Hold up. So you wore these funky draws in the Presence of God in the House of the Lord yesterday?

ME: Again I say, I ain't never really think about it like that, but I—

MOM: I'm gonna tell your daddy.

ME: Woah-woah-woah-woah-woooaaah! Now just wait one got damn minute. Before we go gettin' all irrational about this shit, let's take a deep breath and ask ourselves, do we really need to get Daddy involved in this? I mean, you know how that nigga get.

MOM: (Jerry Springerish) Oh! Whateva! Whateva! Don't get scared now! It's on!

ME: (bold and in denial) Whateva! Go get Daddy! I'm supposed to be scared of him or somethin'? I ain't scared of that nigga! What he gon' do?
(internally) *Oh, Lord, please let him have a heart attack or somethin' before she can tell'em. Think I'm gonna need some backup.*

Hadjii
My House
Brunswick, Georgia 31520

                    Mr. Boogie Man
                    Da Closet
                    In My House, Georgia

June 5, 1984

Mr. Boogie Man
Da Closet
In My House

Dear Mr. Boogie Man,

   Mr. Boogie Man, you have been living in my closet rent-free for several years. I've never invaded your privacy, and you've shown your gratitude by not killing me and I appreciate that. And I hate to bother you on such short notice, because I know you're probably busy scaring other little kids in other closets somewhere, but I was wondering if you would do me a favor. In the likely, and I mean very, very, very, very, very likely event that you're in my closet when my daddy gets home, and for some reason he barges into my room and were to begin to give me one of those beatdowns he's so good at, I was wondering if you would be so kind as to jump out of the closet and whup his ass for me? Please? If you do, I will be your friend. I will even leave all of my army men in the closet for you to play with overnight. Plus, I'll leave some of Daddy's dirty magazines in the closet for you. Deal?

                                    See you around seven,
                                    Hadjii

P.S. Sorry you had to smell those crusty draws all last week.

"The Boogie Man
Ain't Worth a Damn!"

I don't know if I sent that letter to the wrong address, or if I didn't use enough postage, or if the Boogie Man's just a big-ass coward. All I know is he never showed up. Didn't write back or nothin'. Shady.

So I'm just sittin' there waitin' on my ass whuppin or a heart attack, whichever one came first. And being that I was a nonsmoking seven-year-old with the proper blood pressure, it looked like I had a beatdown in my near future. Where's a little cardiac arrest when ya need it? See, y'all don't understand. I was probably about fifty-somethin' pounds and standing at I don't know, one foot five maybe? And my pops was like, six foot five, 240 pounds and, in my humble opinion, had a serious fuckin' chip on his shoulder. He was a real daddy. Ya know what a real daddy is? It's a man that has the God-given ability to strike absolute fear into the heart of his child. It's the stuff that good fathers are made of. It's the quality that makes a kid like myself, who's in the middle of a heated debate with his mother, completely shut the fuck up when he walked into the room.

Kids these days aren't scared of their parents anymore. They get along with their parents. Parents wanna be close to their kids. They're friends now. Parents drink with their kids, they talk about sexual exploits with them, hell, they even say dumb shit like, "Well, at least if he's having sex in my house, I know what he's doing and I can regulate his sexual practices. It's important that we build trusting relationships with our children." Well, my father ain't give a damn about getting along with me.

I was scared shitless of my daddy. Looking back on it, I can kinda understand why he was the way he was. See, he was a big, good-lookin', light-skinned brotha, with good hair. Looked like he might have even had a little Indian in his family. Retired from the military, artistic. You could be sitting on the couch talking to him and he could sketch an exact replica of you before the conversation was over. He also wrote several short stories and things like that, and was damn near brilliant. He would read *Time, Newsweek, Life,* and big-ass novels that most people have in their houses just for decoration, biographies, watch documentaries, etc., and actually retained that shit. He would watch *Jeopardy* and know ALL of the answers. Even Final Jeopardy. And he was a left-handed Scorpio on top of all that! What does that mean? It means, he was fuckin' anal in every sense of the word. Do you know what it's like having a daddy like that? One of those cats who was never wrong or satisfied? Demanded perfection? Excuses are bullshit. Shit ain't never good enough. "I ain't impressed wit'cho dumbass report card even though you got straight A's." "You ain't playin' witcha toys right." "Damn, that's some nappy-ass hair." "Why you ain't got no girlfriend yet? You're ten years old. I was a pimp at your age! You like women, dontcha?" "The big kids took ya ball? Well go out there and getcha ball back. I ain't raisin' no punks." And on and on and on.

And oddly enough, I love him to death for it cause I had standards. Impossible though they were to meet at times, at least I had somethin' to shoot for. But as a kid, the nigga was stressing me out. And trust me, I'm gonna be exaggerating about a lot of shit in this book, but honestly, he was all those things I said above. He was like one of those old wise men in the kung fu movies that keeps sending his protégé on all these goose chases to help him realize his potential. For example, there were times I'd be in my bed asleep and I'd feel his cold stare coming over me in the middle of the night even after a good day where I hadn't done shit wrong, and I'd open my eyes and see his huge, menacing silhouette in my doorway. Then he'd ask me something like, "What's wrong with you?" As if I fuckin' knew? A kid can't answer some shit like that, and even though it was cool in the long run, it's tough on a kid while you're goin' through it. It's enough to make you wanna renegotiate your contract. And what you really have to keep in mind is that he was all those things back in the day. Being a smart, talented, good-looking brotha down south before white folk and black folk got all buddy-buddy. So with that in mind, I say again, he had a SERIOUS fuckin' chip on his shoulder. And everybody out there who had a real father knows that you don't make the king get off the throne, and you definitely don't make a big, intelligent black man with a chip on his shoulder get out of "his chair."

See, every man has his chair. Like, "This is my house. And that's my chair." Nobody sits in Daddy's chair. The only muthafuckas who can sit in Daddy's chair are your grandparents, and they've earned that right because they're old. See, the chair represents power. The chair represents peace. The chair represents control. And when a kid's daddy gets out of the chair, that means things are about to get out of control. Because even the best, most patient, most understanding man can lose control.

I mean, take the great Dr. Martin Luther King, right? Imagine how stressed out he must've been after spendin' all day marching and boycotting on behalf of black people everywhere, black people he didn't even know, only to come home and find his own black children with their toys all over the fuckin' house! "I've been out here in this hot-ass sun marchin' all day and now I gotta come home to this bullshit!" It's enough to drive ya crazy.

And don't get me wrong, my mom on the other hand is one of the nicest, "I love everybody," reading "The Welcome" at church, bringin' macaroni to ya house when ya husband dies, mailing Christmas cards, attending Parent-Teacher Association meetings, bringing cupcakes to school for the Groundhog Day party, picking ya up for work, making spaghetti and toast (my favorite dish as a child), bringin' birthday presents for all your children (even the ones you don't claim), buyin' candy bars from kids trying to pay for their field trip, I'll be praying for ya, visiting the sick, loaning money to the poor women I've ever known. You name it, she'd do it. You know how we all have gifts? Her gift is that she's a good and faithful servant. She extends and gives love like no one else I've ever seen. Matter of fact, her and my daddy used to get in arguments over why she always had to be helpin' somebody. He'd be like, "Why the hell you always gotta be takin' chicken over to somebody's house?" And she'd say, "Cause it's the right thing to do. Besides, everybody likes my chicken." All the little kids at school, even the white ones, used to wish my mama was their mama. And I would think to myself, "Y'all don't know that mufucka like I do." Now don't misunderstand me. I love my mama. But she's got her ways. *Crafty* is a term that comes to mind. Especially when it came to me and my daddy.

My mom was like a biological, diabolical, mad scientist when it came to my daddy. She knew him like the back of her hand. What made it even worse was the fact that she was the only person who could control him, cause I damn sure couldn't. And she knew how to do or not do certain little shit in order to season the ass whuppin to her liking. For example, my mom is a very, very, extremely smart woman. She plays it low-key, but it's an act. She's really an evil mastermind. I've seen her in action. She would've found bin Laden a long time ago. The thing that made her so smart was that she always had the ability to look at things for what they are. Not what they could be or what they might become, but what it is right now. The Bible speaks of a thing called "the gift of a discerning spirit." She's got it down cold! I'm telling you that my mom can meet one of my friends one or two times and pick up on their entire vibe or something. Next thing ya know, she can tell you everything about their history, family background, upbringing, dental records, all that shit. It's fuckin' spooky.

In spite of my father being the complex and quirky perfectionist he was, she knew how to break him down in a manner that made him quite simple. That's how they maintained like a thirty-year marriage until he passed.

She knew that no matter how rich or poor, black or white, smart or dumb, tall or short, ugly or attractive, blah-blah-blah, a man only wants five things out of the day: eat some food, have a few drinks (i.e., relax, for all the nondrinkers out there), watch the game, get some booty, and go to sleep. Period. We don't want no sweaters, we don't wanna talk, we don't wanna reminisce, we don't wanna go to the mall, we don't wanna go to the grocery store, we don't wanna help the kids with their homework, we don't wanna go to the teacher-parent conference, we don't wanna go to open house, we don't wanna go to their play (although we will go to their game; daddies ain't missin' too many of them games—I mean, unless the kid sucks), we don't wanna visit the parents, we don't wanna go over to your friend's house for dinner, we don't wanna go to the funeral, we don't give a fuck about the new baby, we don't wanna send Christmas cards, and Thanksgiving dinner? Just bring us a plate back. BUT we'll do all that stuff if we have to cause we don't want nothing fuckin' up our wife's willingness to give us some food, let us have a few drinks, let us watch the game in peace, gimme some of that good stuff like we used to do before we had this ignorant child of ours, and tuck me in. And my mom knew that, and she didn't care, because she knew my pops, just like any other married man in America, would be satisfied with a forty-sixty split like, "Look, playboy, I gave you food and the game. Now leave me alone." Which was a fair deal as long as he didn't try to keep her from going to the mall, going to see the new baby, etc., etc., it was all good.

You have to understand that even though the man thinks he's the head of the household, every kid knows that Mom's really the one who's runnin' thangs. Cause if Dad's in a bad mood, he comes home and makes things hard on you, the kid, but if Mom's in a bad mood she totally fucks up everybody's day. Now this nigga can't get his forty-sixty split and I can't ride my bike. What the hell is that?

It used to get so bad sometimes that as mean and scary as my daddy was, sometimes I'd get to the point where I'd have to call that nigga into my room for a meeting like, "Look, I don't know what the hell you did to Mama. I guess that ain't really none of my business, but I know you need to apologize or do somethin' cause I can't keep eatin' tuna and cereal every night! I'm fourteen years old and I weigh seventy-three pounds, muthafucka! You need to get this shit right so we can get some steaks back in here!"

So my mom was well aware of the fact that she had the upper hand. So when she wanted to properly "season the ass whuppin," oooh, she could be nasty. This is what she'd do.

SCENE: HOME, EARLY EVENING.
Big black man with a chip on his shoulder is ready to
eat. Nothing's cooked. Nothing's cooking.
DADDY: Uhh? Where's the food?
MAMA: (innocent) I'm sorry. I haven't had time to
    cook. I've been dealing with Hadjii all day.
DADDY: Who's Hadjii?
MAMA: Your son.
DADDY: Oh, him. What's the problem?
MAMA: Oh don't worry about it. Let me fix your
    dinner and everything first. Then we'll talk about it.
    You want a beer?

Note: When seasoning the ass whuppin, alcohol is essential. After a few cold ones:

DADDY: Say, baby, where's the food at? Ya know the
Lakers are about to come on.

MAMA: (depressed) I'm sorry. It's just that . . .
(breaks down)
It's just that Hadjii was yellin' at me today.

DADDY: (furious, cause he's hungry) What?

MAMA: See, I had bought you a big ole T-bone steak,
but then Hadjii put these crusty draws in the
refrigerator and totally contaminated everything!

DADDY: I'll deal with this after the game. Make me
some food without the crusty draws, please.

MAMA: I would, but I'm so distraught I can't
concentrate.

DADDY: But baby—

MAMA: I'm sorry. It's just that dealing with that boy
is taking its toll on me. And I was going to party
with you tonight, but now, I don't even feel sexy.

DADDY: (thinks) Ya know, life would be so much
better if we never had that boy. Maybe I should
kill'em?

MAMA: Well, ya never know until you try.

DADDY: I'll be right back.

SCENE: MY ROOM, EARLY EVENING.

ME: Alright, Boogie Man. He's comin'. You ready?
Boogie Man? Boogie? Boogster? Where are
yoooouuuu? Damn? Can you at least make room
for a nigga in the closet or somethin'?

Hadjii
My House
Brunswick, Georgia 31520

Mr. Boogie Man
Da Closet
In My House, Georgia

June 6, 1984

Mr. Boogie Man
Da Closet
In My House

Dear Mr. Boogie Man,

You ain't shit. I can't believe you just stood there and watched while that nigga tried to kill me! I see why you ain't got no friends. Cause friendship is a give-and-take type of thing, but now I realize that you don't understand that, Mister *Booger* Man. Everybody hates you, including me. You would've liked my army men, but I guess you didn't want that. Maybe some people just ain't ready for the finer things in life. I hope it's nice and cozy in my closet, you punk muthafucka!

You're a doonkie-head,
Hadjii

Like I said, my daddy was crazy, but I survived. What was even crazier was the fact that after I got my beatdown, my mom came in the room and held me in her arms, and my dumb ass was simple-minded enough to hug her back. And then she wiped the tears from my eyes and said some ole comfortin' shit in her soft, sweet voice like, "Didn't I tell you 'bout fuckin' wit' me? Now here's some toilet paper. Let's see if we can do better from here on in. Okay?"

Is This That
"Tough Love" I've
Been Hearing About?

Ya know what some cruel and unusual punishment was? Whenever my mom felt the need to pop one of my bumps. Yes, I said it. My mom used to have to pop bumps on my face, and I know a lot of y'all out there are thinkin' that's the most disgusting thing you've ever heard, but good parents are always doin' a bunch of disgustin' shit that no one in their right mind would volunteer to do like changin' diapers, cleaning noses, and whatnot. Nobody wants to do it, but it's part of the job, and between my crusty draws and acne my mom had to put in overtime. I had a really bad case of acne when I was a kid. I mean really bad. So bad that my folks even had to take me to a dermatologist, like "We gotta get an expert in on this shit." It ended up working itself out eventually, but as a child my mom would find herself thumbing through the phone book on many occasions. Cause before the Internet and all this technological "world at your fingertips" access, the phone book was a muthafucka. Back then, all a nigga needed to get by was a phone book and the right set of encyclopedias. Shit, if you had the right set of encyclopedias you didn't even have to go to college. Britannica was the best institution in the world. And trust me, my mama was always having to look some shit up when it came to me. I say all of that to say this, I hated when my mom got the urge to bust one of my pimples.

I could always see it coming too. We'd be sitting down eating dinner or watching TV or something, and everybody's laughing and having a good time, and then all the sudden I would feel this cold stare locking in on me. Then out of the corner of my eye I could see my mom just sitting there in silence zooming in on one of my pimples. Then in a real businesslike tone she'd say, "Hadjii, come here. No, no, no, wait. Go in the room and bring me my glasses." Remember when you were a kid and your folks always wanted you to bring them some shit from another room that they were too lazy to get up and get for themselves? Bring me the mail. Bring me my purse. Go out there and make something of yourself so you can bring me some money. Remember that? Didn't ya just have the urge to scream at the top of your lungs, "Why don't you go and get it ya fuckin' self?" Butcha never did. At least not where they could hear you. Anyway, your mom tells ya to go in the bedroom and look on the dresser and bring her her glasses. So being the cooperative, accommodating, and generous kid you are, you go in the bedroom, you look on the dresser, and the glasses aren't there. They're never there, are they? So you walk back out and tell her, "I ain't see no glasses, Mama." Then in this case, my mom, who's ready to get her bump-bustin' on, says, "Did you look on the dresser like I told you?" "Yes ma'am." "And you didn't see any glasses?" "No ma'am." "Did you look thoroughly?" "Yes ma'am." "And you didn't see any glasses?" "No ma'am." "Hadjii, if I get up and go in that room and see those glasses on that dresser, I'll be forced to tell your daddy about how you were toying with me again." Then I'd say, "Wait, wait, wait, wait, wait! Lemme look one mo' time." And every single time, whatever they told you to get would be right there where it was supposed to be, but I promise you it wasn't here the first time. I looked. It's that got damn Boogie Man gettin' me back for makin' him stay in the closet with the crusty draws!

So she'd put her glasses on and make me stand under the light, because adults love the light. "Boy cut that light on. Ya can't read wit'out no light. Cut that light on. Ya can't eat in the dark. Turn on the light. Get that boy some light. Get outta my light. Turn off that fan. Gonna run up my light bill." Then my mom would inspect my bump and say, "Oh yeah, this one's ready." Then she'd place her two thumbs on my face and press down on it, and I don't know, I guess I had militant bumps or something, cause it seemed like it took her thirty minutes to pop one sometimes. We'd have to pause in between for lunch breaks. It was rough.

But even though my mom could torture me in her own little way, my dad still found a way to outdo her, cause the worst thing of all times had to be, and I mean *had* to be, when I fucked around and had a loose tooth. Oh hell nah! Because I always thought of my dad as one of the most intelligent people I've ever known, but he got on some real Neanderthal shit when it came to pulling out one of my teeth. His methods were insane. You know how it is. The first time you have a loose tooth it's exciting because you're thinking you're coming into adulthood, ya know. Plus, you've heard all the stories at school about how the Tooth Fairy'll come to your house and break ya off. It's exciting. Then my dad was like, "Well if it's loose, we gotta go 'head and get it! Come 'ere boy and stand in the light." I'm like, "Hell nah. Every time I stand in the light something bad happens. What makes you think I'ma trust you?" But as much as I didn't wanna go over to him, he had a way of *convincing* you that it was the right thing to do. So I go over there and first he had to test it. He put his big-ass adult hands in my little kid mouth and started wiggling my tooth, talkin' about, "Oh yeah. It's loose alright. Go look in the toolbox and bring me my pliers." What?! "No wait. I got a better idea. Come here Hadjii and lemme tie your tooth up to this doorknob and then when I slam the door shut, your tooth's gonna pop right outta there." Nigga, is you crazy? Next thing I know my dad's got his pocketknife out and he's cutting the string off of my yo-yo. "We're almost ready, boy!" I said, "Fuck it. I don't need this shit. I'm runnin' away." Me and my loose tooth packed our bags and hit the mean streets. I think I made it all the way to the mailbox before I stopped and asked myself, "Do I smell spaghetti?" It was at that point that I arrived at a crossroads. "Do I deal with the hunger and starve to death while trying to find my way on the mean streets? Or do I go back inside and let this lunatic pull my tooth out after a nice plate of spaghetti?" Fuck it. The streets ain't so bad.

It was that serious, cause my pops would come up with all these new and innovative ways to get my tooth out. Like, "Hadjii, this is a magnet, and this is the refrigerator. Now opposites attract. So I figure if we get'chou to stand close enough to the door with this magnet in your mouth like so, that tooth oughta jump right outta there. And just in case that doesn't work I've got these pliers handy, which I have strategically attached to the doorknob. Catch my drift?"

For real, man. By the time I was eight I had figured out that there were certain things ya just didn't do in front of certain people. Like you didn't say *ain't* in front of my daddy, cause he'd bark, "Ain't no such word as *ain't*!" And if you ever went over to someone's house for dinner, you'd better eat whatever the hell they were eatin' or else you were actin' like you were better than somebody and my mom didn't play that shit. I remember one time I had to fuck around and eat some pig's feet. Wasn't that bad until somebody told me what it was. Note to adults: Never tell a kid they're eating feet. And one thing I learned that you never-ever-ever-never did was cough, or sneeze, in front of my grandmama. I don't care if somebody sat an entire bottle of black pepper on your top lip, don't sneeze in front of my grandmama. Cause if she thought you were comin' down with somethin', she was gonna try to fix it. And ya know, black people back then when she was growin' up didn't believe in doctors and medicine and stuff like that. They had their own homemade remedies. Like, "Hadjii, sound like you got some frog in ya throat? Come in the kitchen." Now it was bad enough when one of my parents told me to stand in the light, but I'd take that any day over grandmama sayin' "Come in the kitchen!," cause you know somethin' soooo not good is about to happen. She'd go in the kitchen and you'd try to lag behind hoping that in her old age she'd forget she just heard you cough and asked you to come in the kitchen. I quickly learned that when it comes to health grandmamas don't forget a got damn thang.

"Hadjii, I said get in this kitchen!" Oh great. Now I

done pissed her off. Before you even get to the kitchen you can hear the clanging of her sifting through the silverware drawer looking for that old spoon that's been passed down from generation to generation for so many years that it's damn near black now. Then it got even worse, cause she'd pull out the footstool so she could reach some shit that you had tried to hide from her from the last time you got sick at her house. Then she'd reach up in the cabinet and pull out a bottle of castor oil. Castor oil? That's that shit Bugs Bunny and them be drinkin' in the cartoons. "What'chou gonna do with that?" I'd ask. "We gonna clean out'cha system so we can get the devil up outta you."

Then she'd pour some in the spoon and make ya drink it. Now I'm coughin', sneezin', and throwin' up at the same time, and my grandmama would say, "See, that's those demons leavin' his body." And I would be thinkin', "The demons ain't botherin' me. You're the one that's pissin' me off." And if I was stopped up, she'd lean over to my mom and say, "You know what that boy needs? Need to make'em eat some garlic." And my mom was cool. She tried to get me out of it. She'd be like, "Yeah, you're probably right. I'll stop by the store and get some on the way home." Then she'd wink at me like, "You know you owe me one, right? So I don't wanna hear no shit tomorrow when I ask ya to make ya bed." Deal! Then my grandmama would say, "You ain't gotta stop by no store. I got some garlic in the kitchen." Then she'd pull out that fuckin' footstool again. Have you ever eaten some garlic? I ain't talkin' about having some garlic in your food or garlic salt or something. I'm talking about a piece of garlic. Have you ever eaten a piece of garlic? If you haven't, don't! That shit gets in your pores, man. Kids wouldn't play with me for like three days. Dogs would lick my legs, and then be like, "Nigga you stink." Even the Boogie Man was like, "I'll see ya next week." It's a good safety precaution though, cause after you eat a few pieces of garlic, you ain't gotta worry about anybody tryin' to kidnap ya. That's for sure. You got a kid and you want them to hang on to their virginity? Make'em eat some garlic a few times a week. That's a contraceptive for yo ass.

Now if you haven't gotten the picture by now, my father, although I love'em to death, wasn't exactly the nicest person in the world. I think I've made that point clear. But as cold as he could be, he ain't have shit on my granddaddy. Woo! Talk about crazy! Now don't misunderstand me. My granddaddy was one of the most charismatic people I've ever known. Everybody loved my granddaddy. Everybody respected him too. Now that I'm older I realize a lot of people were just straight up scared of that nigga.

He was a nice guy. Smooth, good sense of humor, loved the Lord, was about six foot three or somethin', and made pretty good money for a black man back then, but talk about a temper. You ever been around one of those people who *snap*? Know what I'm talkin' about? People who can just be sittin' there and everything's fine, and then you say the wrong thing and they fly off the fuckin' handle? My granddaddy was like a nuclear time bomb. My granddaddy was so scary he ain't even have to hit us. We were always on our best behavior 'round that dude cause we knew there weren't any limits to what he was capable of. He was an old tough type. I'm talkin' about that old-school rough and rugged black John Wayne shit. We'd be walking through the woods or somethin' and you know how you might see a big-ass spiderweb with a huge tarantula in it or somethin'? He'd just walk right through it like it wasn't even there. I don't think the dude was scared of shit. He'd pick a snake up by his head and be like, "What the fuck are you doin' in my yard? Get on from 'round here!" and throw that bitch somewhere. He was nuts! And he ain't take too kindly to people disagreeing with him either, especially a kid. And as far as kids went, he ain't want shit done now. He wanted shit done *right* now. He was one of them cats that would get mad and ask you a question that you better not try to answer. His eyes would turn red and bulge like they were about to pop outta his face and he'd scream at the top of his lungs at'cho ass and you'd just sit there and take it in complete silence, and you better not get caught breathing too loud cause that was almost like talkin' back. That cat was cold, man, but he always had a dollar.

When we were kids (I say *we* meaning my cousins and myself), every time we saw him he'd give us a dollar. When I was little-little I used to ball his dollar up and be like, "I don't want it." (Even back then I realized money was just an apparatus used by Da Man to control my mind.) But by the time I turned seven or eight and realized that those dollars could be used to play video games I changed my tune. Plus, he really was a cool dude. He'd pick me up and sit me on top of his shoulders and walk me around and shit. And when all of us cousins were together, he'd beat all of us up. He'd be sittin' in his chair (I told y'all before, every man has "his chair") and all of us would charge him and try to hit him and he would kick our ass. He was an old-school cat that had one of those grips that when he grabbed you, it raised your blood pressure. He'd be holdin' this one, kicking that one, slappin' that one, and choking me all at the same time. And you know what? It was fun as hell. And he'd be talkin' shit while he was doin' it too. He'd say stuff like, "I'm much of a man!" and "I'll whip a cow-pen full of ya!" and "I'm strong like an oxen!" and "The bear gotcha!" Who ever knew gettin' ya ass kicked could be so amusing?

Then you had my grandmama. She probably stood at only like five feet tall on her tiptoes. I mean, once she took her heels off she was barely above sea level. And she was a nice lady, but you talkin' about a little woman that could hand out an ass whuppin? Give my grandmama a belt and she turned into Zorro. She ain't beat us much. Actually she only beat us once, but after she did it once, trust me, the tone had been set. Cause you know how kids are. Especially boys. Granddaddy would be off at work or something and we'd be there with Grandmama and she'd be like, "Y'all stop throwin' them rocks at each other." And we'd be like, "Yeah whatever. Shut'cho little munshkin ass up." Cause she wasn't much bigger than us, plus we had her outnumbered, so we figured we could take her if it ever came down to it. Shiiit. Another rock flew and I guess God gives old women supernatural powers or somethin' cause my grandmama flew off that porch and started Bruce Leein' niggas. You know it's fucked up when your mom comes to pick you up and she's like, "Damn! Look like y'all caught a bad one." Cause men can talk all the shit they want to about how they'll kick somebody's ass or how fast they can knock somebody out, blah-blah-blah, but trust me, you ain't truly seeeeen no ass whuppin till you witnessed an old black woman get hold of a little kid. They put their hands on yo ass! I think it's part of some overall plan though, cause they whoop you so nasty that you actually develop a new appreciation for your parents. You go home thinking, "Ya know? Y'all ain't that bad. I'm just glad I don't have to live with Grandmama crazy ass."

I think they actually get off on beatin' kids up cause they can take discipline to a whole new level. Old black women can beat you so bad you feel like you can damn near relate to what the slaves went through. Like my mom would call to check on me, right? And it seems like she always knew to call right after I got a beatin'. One of the maternal things, I guess? Cause she'd call and talk to grandmama for a minute. Then I'd get a chance to talk to her and it would go something like this . . .

ME: (whispering) Hello?

MOM: Hey.

ME: (nervous) Mama? Is that'chou?

MOM: Yeah, who'd you think it was?

ME: (whispering) Shhh! Don't talk too loud. Else Grandmama might hear us. I sho' is afraid here at da bighouse. Dis moanin' granny dun woke us up out our sleepness, and make us git out in da garden ta do her biddins. Thangs was good at furst. Den I, I mean somebody dun went and dug up a 'mato fo' its time come! Oh Granny was helluh-mad! She wint ta fussin' and cussin' up somethin' awful! Uh-oh! I gotta go! She's a comin'!

But she was cool most of the time. She only got bad when she blew up, and nothing could make her blow up more than that one thing that makes every old black woman lose it. Bad report card? No. Breaking something in the house? No. Concealed weapons charge? Nope. The thing that used to send my grandmama over the edge was kids coming in and out of the house. She couldn't stand that shit. We'd all be over at her house for dinner or something and we'd wanna go outside and play. That was fine, but then somebody would get thirsty and run inside to get something to drink. Then somebody would run inside to use the bathroom and then go back out. Then somebody would run inside to grab a snack. Then somebody would run inside to ask their mama some-thing. Then somebody would run inside to tell on somebody. Then somebody would run inside to—and all of the sudden my grandmama would catch that one unfortunate nigga and say, "Sit'cho ass down! Y'all little bastards either stay inside or outside! Matter of fact! Fuck it! Everybody, get in here right now! And shut the door! Y'all lettin' all the cold air out!"

However, the cool thing about my grandmama was she always had food. You could go over to my grandparents' house four o'clock in the morning and she'd be like, "Y'all hungry?" "No, Grandmama." Next thing ya know pots would start clanging and five minutes later you had a meal in front of ya. And you better eat it too!

Now my grandparents stayed out in the woods, which we called "the country." I'm talkin' about that old-school country where your nearest neighbor lives two miles down the road. The country. Nothing but trees, possums, armadillos, and gators. So whenever we spent the night at our grandparents' house it was always interesting. It would be four of us in this queen-sized bed and there weren't any streetlights or stuff like that out there so when you turned off the lights, you really turned off the lights. You couldn't see shit. The room would be so dark you couldn't see your hand in front of your face. Then my oldest cousin, who was a real asshole (I mean he had to be, cause he was the oldest), would start his bullshit.

"Who's gonna sleep on the edge of the bed? Cause if a burglar comes in, he's gonna kill whoever's on the edge first. But whoever sleeps by the wall's gonna be the last one to get out." You know that dumb shit used to always work, cause me and the second-youngest cousin would always end up sleepin' in the middle. Just in case. Then he'd start talkin' shit about "Bloody Mary." For those of you who don't know, before that movie *Candyman* came out, before Freddy Krueger and *A Nightmare on Elm Street*, and before Jason, there was Bloody Mary. Legend has it, and I don't know how this bitch died, or why she's so pissed off, but if you stand in the mirror and say "Bloody Mary one," and then spin around and say "Bloody Mary two," and then spin around again and say "Bloody Mary three," and then spin around again, and keep doin' that shit until you get to ten, this bloody woman is gonna pop up behind you and fuck you up.

Now I don't know if the shit's true or not, but I know that I've been on this earth for a long time and I didn't get this far by tempting fate. To this day I have never gone all the way to ten, and have no intentions on ever goin' all the way to ten. Plus, nowadays, with our microwave society, she'll probably jump on ya by the time you get to four. But my cousin, like I said, he's the oldest so he had to be the jerk, would go all the way up to nine . . . and then be like, "Fuck it! Bloody Mary ten!" Then jump in the bed with us like, "If she comes to get me, she gotta kill y'all too!" Ain't that some selfish shit? I'm seven years old. I'm cryin' like a muthafucka and this nigga thinks he's sooooo funny. Then my grandmama would open the door and say, "Y'all hush that fuss!" and we would shut the fuck up. We don't want another Zorro incident. And my grandmama was a trip too, cause she'd

wake up like six in the morning. Then she'd come wake
us up. You'd be like, "It's still dark outside. What the hell
is your problem?" and she'd order us, "Y'all put on ya
clothes and help ya granddaddy in the yard!" Trust me.
Nothin' can fuck up a kid's Saturday like the damn yard.

Ya ever wake up on a Saturday mornin' lookin' for-
ward to hanging out, playing, or doing whatever it is you
wanna do, only to find out that your dad or somebody's
already got your entire Saturday planned for you? To a
kid, there's nothing worse. It never failed. On the nicest
day of the year, the one Saturday where all of the fun shit
was going to happen like a friend's pool party or somethin', my mom would get the urge to plant a flower bed.
I hated them muthafuckin' flower beds with a passion!
We'd go to Wal-Mart and I'd see them little cheap trays
of flowers over in the corner and I'd be thinking, "Okay,
I gotta distract her. Can't let her make eye contact with
the flowers. "Hey Mama. Let's go look at the bicycles."
Damn it! She saw'em. She'd buy a couple of trays of
flowers. Some white ones, some red ones, some pink
ones, some yellow ones, etc., and some soil, and then
she'd get some of them little tools, I don't know whatcha
call'em, but it's like a minishovel and a minipitchfork,
and then next thing ya know, we'd be farmin' the land,
buddy. Mosquitoes tearing half my flesh away, but she
don't give a damn, and I'm thinkin', "God, can a brother
get some rain, please? I wanna go inside! Helloooo?" But
the rain never came, unless of course it was a Saturday
where you ain't have no chores at all. Then it was gonna

rain like hell. Nothing cuts a kid deeper than a rainy Saturday. "You mean I can't go outside? Well can I at least just go down the street? Can I check the mail? Sit on the porch? Hey daddy, I'll even read those encyclopedias ya gave me for my birthday if ya lemme read'em on the porch. I just wanna go outside!"

And then there was one summer where it got to a point where we couldn't even go outside anymore for a while because some guy in Atlanta started kidnapping everybody's kids. Man, he had everybody (or at least all the parents worth their salt) shook to death. That dude single-handedly changed every kid in my neighborhood's life. You used to be able to ride your bike down the street. Not anymore, buddy. Now you could only ride your bike from the car to the mailbox, and maybe in the backyard if it was fenced in. That is unless of course your parents were honest enough to let you know that nobody wanted you so you weren't worth kidnapping.

But remember the good ole days when your mom was just runnin' in the store for a minute and you could wait in the car? Well this dude completely took that from me, because now I had to go in every sickening department store with my mama just to be on the safe side, and this changed the way my mom shopped because she used to have to rush because she had a kid in the car. Now, since I'm going in with her, she'll only be in for a "minute or two," which always ended up turning into at least half of my day. (Note to my woman: That's why I hate shopping to this day. See, a man goes into a store to see if that store has what he wants. A woman goes into a store to see if she wants anything that store has. Know what the difference is? About an hour and forty-five minutes.) I think those days have traumatized me, because I still hate shoppin' with my woman. I mean, I refuse to go shoppin' with my woman.

And it took a while, but I finally got my girl to the point where she doesn't even ask me if I wanna go anymore, and I thought I was off the hook until I realized that even though I didn't go shopping with her, I've still gotta sit through that corny-ass fashion show women like to put on when they get home from a successful day on the prowl.

Every man knows about the fashion show. That's where your lady tries everything on, models it for you, gives you the history of the outfit, what makes it so special, and of course, where she plans to wear it. This shit usually takes about four days. "Hadjii! Look at this dress. Do you like it? This is a Millia Milanicia dress. They don't even make these anymore, especially ones with the velvet! Do you know how much these things cost? This is just like the one J-Lo had on at the Golden Globes! Of course she had diamonds on hers and these are rhinestones, but isn't it sharp? There was this other girl in there tryin' to get to it before me, but you know I wasn't havin' that. I tapped her on the shoulder and said, 'Excuse me, but your shoe's untied, and when she looked down I pepper-sprayed that bitch!'"

However, the only thing that made shoppin' somewhat okay when I was young was the fact that you used to get to stay in the car. I could do this when we had one of my cousins with us, because I guess she figured nobody in their right mind would be dumb enough to kidnap two niggas. Me and my cousin loved stayin' in the car, but under one condition. She had to leave us the keys. Soon as she'd hit the door we'd turn the radio on, get it off the gospel station, and turn to the closest thing we had to a black station. In other words, they played Men at Work and Duran Duran, but every now and then they'd fuck around and play Michael Jackson or Prince. It was only once every four hours, but fuck it. We liked those odds cause that's how long she was gonna be in the store anyway. We'd sit in that hot-ass car for hours. And just for the record, cars used to be hot as hell back then. They had like that plastic interior in cars that wasn't suede, but it damn sure wasn't leather. It was like sittin' on a heating pad. Like even the steering wheel and the dashboard used to get hot. And we used to have on them little coochie-cutter-ass shorts so the heat off the seats would be burnin' the back of our legs and had our thighs all black and shit. Those cars used to get hot! Then a Stevie Wonder song would come on and you'd get so excited you'd forget how hot them radio dials could get and burn the shit outta ya fingers when you tried to turn it up.

And it's funny, because every now and then we'd be able to pick up a black radio station, and even though I was only a kid I began to notice some really funny things about race, because we always listened to white stations most of the time because that's all we could pick up on our radio, so we were used to hearing the radio commercials that were aimed at their white audience. But when we got a chance to hear a company do a commercial that was aimed at their black audience it would be completely different. They'll make *these* commercials to address the white audience, then they'll make *deez* commercials to address the black audience. What's wrong with that? Nothing really, except for the fact that the black commercials always make us look like a bunch of fuckin' idiots.

Example: Let's say a fast-food restaurant (restaurant, soft drink, and alcohol commercials are the biggest culprits when it comes to this), ya got a fast-food restaurant, let's name it "Hadjii Burger." No, y'all deserve more. Let's name it "Affluence Burger."

Alright, so here's an example of the radio spot for Affluence Burger on a white station . . .

SETUP: *A kid, her mother, and her mother (the kid's grandmother) are riding in a car together.*
KID: Mommy, Mommy! There's an Affluence Burger! Can we stop, Mommy, please-huh-pleeeease?
MOTHER: No, Heather, we'll be late for ballet. Besides, all those fast-food places are bad for you.
GRANDMOTHER: That's not so.
MOTHER: Well, that's what you always told me when I was growing up.
GRANDMOTHER: I know, but that was before I discovered Affluence Burger. They aren't like other

burger joints. They only use the world's best beef
straight from virgin Midwestern cows, the fries are
all fried in pure vegetable oil, and the prices are to
die for. That's why it's called Affluence Burger. It's
fast food for those who want the finer things in life
while simultaneously maintaining financial excellence.

KID: Not to mention the rich and juicy taste!

GRANDMOTHER: Everything on the menu is low in
carbs and the service is so fast and efficient that
we'll be in and out of there before you can say
prosperity.

KID: What's that word mean?

MOTHER: That means, "We're stopping at Affluence
Burger."

KID: Yeah!

ANNOUNCER: Affluence Burger. Fast food for those
who want the finer things in life.

Now before we go any further let's touch on a few
points I want you to notice about that advertisement. Did
you see all that information in there? See how they guided
that one toward the kids and the family? Generation to
generation? Affluence and health and prosperity? Now
tell me what you see in the next one.

SETUP: *A black man and a black woman in the hood.*

TWON: Yo-yo-yo-yo what's poppin', shorty? What's
yo name?

SHANIKWA: Shanikwa, but before you even waste

yo time tryin' to git wit' me, you need to know dat
I'm lookin' for a balla.

TWON: Yo word?

SHANIKWA: Skraight up.

TWON: Well lemme kick my credentials to ya. I'm a
twenty-one-year-old ad executive who's about to
make partna, I don't live wit' my mama, I take care
of all my kids, and I know how to please a strong
black woman.

SHANIKWA: And just how do you do that, playa-
playa?

TWON: By takin'em to Affluence Burger.

SHANIKWA: Oooh! I dun hurd about dat place!
Over on Tenf Skreet. I hurd dey got all dem fancy
sammiches, but at unfancy prices.

TWON: Yeah, it's where all the ballas and shotcallas
go to get they grub on. Da food is off da heezy for
sheezy, they ain't skimpy wit' da cheezy—

SHANIKWA: Are the fries greazy?

TWON: Please believe meeeeeeeeeeeeee! Gurl, da
food is so good it's gonna make yo badonkadonk
even mo' badonkier!

SHANIKWA: Well whut is we waitin' on? Let's go.

A car cranks up. A man leans out of the window and
hollers to Shanikwa.

JAMAAL: Shanikwa, a Shanikwa, where you goin'?

TWON: Who's dat?

SHANIKWA: Dat's my man. I mean . . . dat used to be my man! I'm rollin' wit'chou!

ANNOUNCER: Affluence Burger. Fast food for those who like to bling-bling.

SINGER: (sings) Affluence Burga . . . When you wanna bling!

ANNOUNCER: Located on Tenth Street next to Kim Li's Nail Shop right before you get to the railroad tracks.

The Family

Function

Now I came from one of those families that was the event family. Like my aunts and uncles would always have family functions where they'd invite all kinds of people over and have dinner or some crab-boil, seafood feast, or whatever. Notice I said my aunts and uncles? We never held shit at our house, cause my daddy wouldn't ever let anybody in. Anyway, these functions would usually consist of family, friends, maybe a few church folks, a few distant relatives who just sit on the sofa and are always ready to leave, and a couple of really old people who your mom thinks it's important for you to meet before they die.

Now to us kids, these functions were just a chance for us to get together and play or hang out, but to the adults these functions were like really important, because "the family's got to stick together." And "you don't know where ya goin' unless ya know where ya come from." And "you can snap a branch, but ten branches stuck together are unbreakable." And a whole bunch of other dumb shit that people say when they ain't got no money.

Anyway, our functions were cool, because I liked being around my family, but what used to fuck the gatherings up would be those friends-of-the-family people, because they'd come over and get a little too comfortable too quickly. Like that overweight woman that all kids hate. You know the one overweight lady that comes over and finds the nicest chair in the house and then stays in that mufucka all day? She doesn't offer anybody any help, she doesn't bring any food with her, she doesn't offer to help clean up afterward or anything. All she does is harass little kids. Because you don't know her name, you don't know who she's related to, you don't even know where she came from, but every time you walk by that lady she's askin' you to do something for her. Hadjii, bring me back some water. Hadjii, bring me back some tea. Hadjii, you'll go in the kitchen and get me some of that pie? Hadjii, take my plate. Hadjii, where's the ashtray? Bring it here. Hadjii, go in the back room and bring me my purse. Hadjii, you mind goin' out to the car and bringin' back my readin' glasses? Hadjii, you mind goin' in the bathroom and bringin' me the toilet? Oh, I'm sorry. I didn't know you were eating. Hadjii, lemme taste that.

And what makes it even worse is they thank Jesus for everything. And I mean everything. Which is cool, but I'd bring'er back a glass of water, and she'd take a sip and say, "Umm. Thank ya Jesus." And I'm eight years old thinkin', "Bitch, I'm the nigga that went in the kitchen. Can I get some credit?"

Then ya get older and your duties change. It used to be "Hadjii, go in the kitchen." But now it's "Hadjii, go to the store." And there's always that one middle-aged forty- or fifty-year-old dude named Joe or somethin' who's down on his luck, so somebody brought him over just so he could eat and hang out, because losers need love too.

But Joe's cool. You know how people are when they're invited for dinner around a family. He's friendly, somewhat reserved. Just trying to fit in. So he's there watching the game with your uncles, and they're making him feel welcomed. Everything's cool, but when the game reaches halftime he stands up and asks, "Can somebody run me to the store real quick?" Whatcha need? "Oh, nothin', nothin'. I just need to go to the store for a minute." Then all of the sudden everyone acts overly concerned and begins to give him a thousand and one reasons why he shouldn't go to the store. "There's drinks in the fridge. There's beer in the cooler. Whatcha need?"

Joe says, "Nothin' much. I just need to get some stuff."
Then more reasons he shouldn't go begin to fly. "The
food'll be ready in a minute. By the time you get back the
food'll be cold. The second half's about to start. It's dark
outside. Looks like rain. You don't wanna go out in this
part of town. Police'll harass ya. It's gangs. There're
terrorists out there. Wolves. Herpes." And I'd be sittin'
there like, "Damn, I'm never going to the store again.
That shit is dangerous." And of course that's when someone says, "Yeah man, you ain't gotta go to the store. We'll
make Hadjii do it. He's expendable."

But for some strange reason Joe won't let you go to
the store by yourself. Instead he insists on riding with
you. So now I'm riding down the street with an absolute
stranger while also on the lookout for tigers and whatnot
and it's a little weird. So in order to break the ice I try to
get a little small talk going, but he doesn't respond. He
just keeps mumbling to himself as if he were in deep
thought and wiggling his finger like he's figuring numbers in his head. As a result this gets my brain in gear, because now I'm thinkin', "Hmm, just why are we goin' to
the store anyway? What exactly is this must-have item
that we're out here risking our lives for?"

So finally we get to the store, walk inside, and can ya
guess what Joe wanted? Can ya guess what Joe is risking
our lives over? A bunch of got damn scratch-off tickets!

"Gimme five Quick Picks, seven Powerballs, eleven
Easy Eights, nine Jumbo Bucks, twelve Lucky Donkeys,
three Sexy Sevens, four Million-Dollar Scholars, two

Blackjacks, twenty-two Fantasy Fives, fifty-nine Poker-faces, nineteen Full Houses, forty-three Instant Cashes, some Georgia Lottos, a couple of Florida Lottos, two Hawaii Lottos, eighteen Canada Lottos, and thirteen Flirtatious Fives boxed."

And now the same dude who's been quiet, reserved, and composed all day is sitting in my passenger seat frantically scratching off lottery tickets like a madman. But it gets even worse, because now that same quiet, reserved, and composed dude who wouldn't say a word to me going to the store, now wants to talk my back out about what he's going to do with the money once he hits.

"Yeah, I heard it's up to sixty-seven million tonight! I could use sixty-seven million! You know what I'd do wit' sixty-seven million dollars? I'd do sixty-seven million thangs, youngun! First of all, I'd get outta debt! Shit, pay for them hospital bills and that mufuckin' wide-screen TV! Then I'd buy me a couple of tigers! Ya know when ya got that kinda money, mufuckas'll try to break in ya house wantin' to take whatcha got, but I betcha a few tiger claws up they ass'll cut that shit short! I guarantee ya that! Then I'd reconcile wit' my wife. Ya know, Delores been good to me. If I hit that jackpot tonight, I think she'd deserve a couple hundred dollars to make up for the time I spent our mortgage on them slot machines. Our credit ain't been right ever since. Maybe give'er a couple hundred dollars and take'er to dinner at Red Lobster or somethin'? Sixty-seven million oughta cover that. I mean just imagine it. I go from driving the school bus to hanging out wit' Bill Gates and that King Tut mufucka! Matter of fact, if I hit, I wouldn't even quit my job! That's the mistake most niggas make. They quit they job. That's how ya go broke! Instead of just havin' sixty-seven million, I'd keep workin' and have sixty-seven million and three hundred dollars! Gotta keep that income comin' in.

"Shit, much stress as them muthafuckas done put me through, I'll keep my job just to get on they fuckin' nerves. Boss'll come in like, "Joe! Get to work," and I'll say, "Boss! Get these nuts, beeiutch!" Cause you can speak ya mind when ya got sixty-seven million dollars! Plus, besides just workin', I'd set a few thousand dollars aside and invest it. Pump that money back into buyin' somethin' lucrative. Like more scratch-offs. Then I'd go and do some more reconcilin' wit' my daughter. She's thirty-seven now and I never really took the time out to get to know'er, and ain't nothin' more important than that father-daughter relationship, so maybe I'd shoot'er a couple hundred dollars and take her to Red Lobster too. That oughta cover it.

"And even though I know gamblin's wrong in the eyes of God and I know the Lotto's a form of gamblin', I still done promised Jesus. Lawd, if ya let me win, I gotcha! Give God a couple hundred dollars and a trip to Red Lobster. He'll get over it."

But there were a lot of times where the family got together and we had a special guest. Someone who I like to refer to as the Old Man in the Room. See, I've got one of those aunts who likes to search for relatives on the Internet so she's always bringing home all kinds of random old people like stray dogs and shit. So nobody really knows who this dude is, but apparently this is my great-great-great granddaddy's cousin or somethin'.

Everybody's sitting around talking, eating, watching the game, having a good time, and then everybody has to stop everything they're doing because the Old Man in the Room wants to say some shit. Now there's a difference between your grandfather and the Old Man in the Room. Your granddaddy's earned the right to say whatever he wants whenever he wants. But nobody really cares about what the Old Man has to say, because nobody knows who the Old Man is, and nobody really gives a shit, but at the same time, the Handbook clearly states that it's bad luck to tell old people to shut the fuck up.

And since the Old Man is the oldest person there, he has to say the blessing over the food, but his memory's not too good.

OLD MAN: Good bread
　　Good meat
　　Good Lawd
　　Let's uhh . . .
SOMEBODY: Let's eat.
OLD MAN: Yeah, let's eat or chow down or sthome sthit.
SOMEBODY: So Old Man, where you from?
OLD MAN: I don't know. Anyway . . . (quickly)

What's the name of that movie wit' da drummer
boy and da sthingin' and dancing and everybody
havin' a good time, but da drummer boy ain't that
friendly?

SOMEBODY: *Drumline.*

OLD MAN: Yeah, *Drumsticks* or sthome sthit. I liked
that one part where they cut da drummer boy foot
off cause he wouldn't change his Aftrican name to
Tobie. He liked bein' called "Coochie-Coo" or
sthome sthit.

SOMEBODY: Ya mean *Roots.*

OLD MAN: No, I think I'm still talkin' 'bout
Drumsticks. Anyway, white people sure used to be
uptight. I remember this one time I was on da bus
and they tried to make this one lady sit in da back
wit' da rest of us, but she wanted a window seat or
sthome sthit. Then everybody got mad and we all
had to start walkin' everywhere.

SOMEBODY: You were on the bus with Rosa Parks?

OLD MAN: No, I was on the bus at Central Park, but
we mighta passed a Rose Park. Wasn't payin' much
attention.

SOMEBODY: No. I meant were you a part of the
civil rights movement?

OLD MAN: Oh yeah, I love civil rights time. All ya
family and friends come around and sthing civil
rights carols and put presents under the civil rights
tree, and Santa Closet makes his speech about a
dream or sthome sthit.

SOMEBODY: That's Christmas.

OLD MAN: Oh, you wanna hear 'bout my birthday?
Well, I was born in a small town outside of
Maryland called Bethlehem. Everybody was real
excited to see me too, cause they brought me
special gifts like frankincense, and gold, and
mirrors.

SOMEBODY: That's Jesus.

OLD MAN: Who?

SOMEBODY: Jesus. Ya know? Bethlehem? Gold?
Wise men?

OLD MAN: Ya know, I think you're right? I get the
two of us mixed up all the time. Ya know I damn
near drowned tryin' to walk on water once.

But as annoying and irritating as all of those people
could be, they ain't got shit on this last guest. This is ya
mom's or aunt's friend from the church. Ya know how
women have always got that one friend that's really a char-
ity case? And you've met her a couple of times and she's a
nice enough lady. She's trying her best to be a strong, inde-
pendent black woman, but for some reason something's
always getting in the way. That is, up until now, because
she's reading her Bible and watching *Oprah*. Therefore
she is about to have her Breakthrough Year.

It usually happens like this. Everyone's eaten dinner,
people have made their take-home plates, and most of all
the normal people who actually have lives of their own
have gone home. Not the Breakthrough Lady. She's just

sitting there waiting on her chance to make her proclamation of change and what God's goin' to do for her this
year.

Then someone will say something like, "Well, this
sure has been fun. We have to do this again sometime."
And that's when the Breakthrough Lady chimes in with
some unrealistic bullshit that's never gonna happen, like
"Ya know, by this time next year, I'll be able to invite all
of y'all to my house for dinner on me!" And everybody's
sitting there like, "Yeah right, whatever." But your mom
invited the chick and she doesn't want her to be embarrassed, so she'll respond with something like, "That's
right, girl. You've gotta believe it to achieve it." Or some
other upliftin' shit that nice women say to people who
ain't got no money.

And then the Breakthrough Lady would go on to say:
"That's right, girl, because that's what it's all about!
Maximizing your opportunities! See, that's my resolution
for the new year! To take advantage of every opportunity
my sweet Jesus sets before me! Cause see the Lord done
told ya you already have the victory! For every one step
you take, he'll take two! You just gotta stick with it!
I just got finished readin' this book called *Taking
Advantage of Your Opportunities* and I am convinced
that *this* is gonna be my year! I'm claimin' it! No more
debt! No more sickness! I'm gonna fix the problems in
my household! I'm gonna get my finances in order! And
I'm takin' control of my circumstances! God made me to
be the head and not the tail! This year I'm taking on the

role of leadership in my family! Leadership in my church! Leadership at my job! And leadership in my community! That devil better stop fuckin' wit' me cause I ain't tryin' to hear none of his bullshit this year! I ain't listenin' to that spirit of doubt! I ain't hearin' his spirit of rejection! Neglect! None of that shit! And whenever he come tryin' to get in my head I'ma tell that devil, 'Devil! You better get the hell on 'fore I whup yo ass!' I'm takin' my family back! I'm takin' my finances back! Devil! Get'cho hands off it, you can't have it! Keep on fuckin' wit' me, I got somethin' for yo ass! For this is Alice's year! Just the other day, I was watchin' this documentary about P. Diddley! You like P. Diddley? Well, I never liked P. Diddley before I watched this special, but he is one in-spirational muthafucka! Lemme tell ya! Do you know he came from nothin'? Nothin'! And now he's a multimil-lionaire! Multi! Know why? Cause he wouldn't take no for an answer! He didn't let the bullshit stop'em! He never gave up! P. Diddley always saw the light at the end of the tunnel! He's reminiscent of Moses and the Red Sea! He kept on goin' and goin' even though the water was red, and that's what I'ma do! I'm gonna find the P. Diddley in me! The Bible says we all have gifts! I can't sing. I can't dance. My mental capacity may not be what others would expect from me, but I make some hellafied brownies! Maybe I should open a restaurant? That's what P. Diddley would do!

"And I know what you're thinkin'. You're thinkin', 'Alice? It's easy for you to speak so boldly cause you multitalented. You multitaskededed. You're an exceptional sista.' But no, I'm not an exceptional sista. I'm just a sista who does exceptional thangs! Oooh! I wish that punkass devil would come in my face wit' that bullshit! See, the devil wanna try to stick his pitchfork up yo ass! But my ass is covered by the blood of the smooth and powerful Jesus Suave! Devil can't get nothin' here! Messin' 'round wit' me, the devil'll fuck around and get saved! I don't play that shit!

"I'm so confident that you wanna know what I did yesterday? Yesterday I set my waitress uniform on fire and bought sixteen business suits! Cause I ain't waitin' on nobody this year! I'm finna take what God's been holdin' for me! I'ma strong-arm fear! I'ma arm-wrestle wit' doubt! And I'ma beat the dog shit outta lack! Cause now I know who I am! I done made contact wit' the P. Diddley in me! This is the year that I get my Oprah on! Yesterday when I was watchin' *Oprah* I got my camera out the closet! And I took a picture of Oprah and them diamonds she be wearin' in 'er ears! And I hung that picture in my bathroom! And every day since yesterday while I was getting ready to open up my brownie-making business I started focusing on them diamonds, and I said, "Bitch! You gonna be takin' a picture of the diamonds in my ear tomorrow!" Not that I'm materialistic, but I want me some materialistic shit! Not for the sake of blinging, but just to illustrate what my almighty God can do! Oh, how I love you, sexy Jesus!

"So for the rest of y'all in here, who invited me over

and prepared this fine feast, and will hopefully let me take some food, I'd like to leave you with some words of encouragement. I'd like to leave you with a message. A message of love! A message of faith! A message of strength! Be strong! Be courageous! Be of good cheer! Live without fear! Be the head and not the tail! Locate your inner P. Diddley and take pictures of Oprah! Live every day as if it were your last! But plan every day like you gonna live forever! Shoot for the moon! Cause even if you miss you'll be among the stars!"

And by this time even my mom was exhausted, but she'd still try to come up with some cool shit to say like, "Okay." To which Alice would reply, "Good . . . Now can somebody give me a ride home?"

"Is It Sunday Again?"

Now before we go any further let's get one thing straight. I love the Lord! Lord knows I do! If anybody tries to come between me and the Lord I'ma have to cut'em. And if it was me, I would have to cut myself. But I know the Lord wouldn't like that. Now that we all have that understanding, I hope that nobody finds these next words to be blasphemous, but I couldn't stand church when I was a kid. Don't get me wrong. It was cool at first, cause when you're a kid-kid, like a toddler or somethin', ya mom would let you take a few toys to church, you play for a while, eat some lemonheads and red-hots, then fall asleep. That ain't a bad day. But once you hit about six or seven and your mom starts expecting you to actually pay attention and listen and stuff, church starts to suck, cause it always seemed to me like it was just a bunch of old black people talking about dying. Trust me, nobody loves dying more than old black people. They talk about "When I'm dead and gone. When my body rots up. When the worms come to eat of my flesh." Used to scare the fool outta me cause I was like, "Worms gonna eat me?" Yeah, I know I'll be dead, but that's besides the point. I hate worms.

Sundays were a trip. And every week would be a new adventure, because I hated going to church so much that every Sunday I would try to come up with a new way to get out of having to go. Even if it meant putting my life on the line. See, there were two or three things my parents always stressed to me. Number one was respect. You respect other people and you respect their property. I dare you to walk into a room full of adults and forget to speak. Oh hell nah! So respect was one. Then, on top of that, my mom stressed church and spirituality and my dad stressed education. Not to say my mom didn't care about education. That would be far from the truth, but my mom felt like (a) Jesus'll make ya smart, and (b) it's better to be dumb in heaven than burnin' in hell wit' a doctorate. But my dad, man, he pushed education hard. I remember the first time I brought home a C on my report card. I was scared as hell. I was probably in like seventh grade and my mom, bless her heart, I showed it to her, and my mom always had a trick she used on report card day. She'd look at the grade and if it was anything less than an A she'd look over at the conduct grade. If I made a B with unsatisfactory conduct that meant I could've made an A if I hadn't've been cuttin' up. But if the conduct was good and I just made a bad grade she'd look at me with those warm and lovin' eyes and ask, "Do you really think you did the best you could?" and I'd be like, "Yeah, Mama, but it's that mythology shit. Zeus just be kickin' a nigga ass, man. So, what's for dinner?" But my pops wasn't quite as understandin'. I'd show him my grades and he'd be like, "What's with the C?" And as I shook my head in shame (trying to create that Hallmark moment) I'd say, "Hey, I did my best," and he'd say, "Boy, you're twelve years old. You don't even know what your fuckin' best is yet. *I'll* tell you when you've done your best!"

So there'd be a lot of times where I'd have a report or science project or something due for school and I'd put it off until the last minute. Then Sunday morning would roll around and then I'd be sitting at the dining room table with like five encyclopedias and index cards and all that stuff ya use when you're tryin' to make it look like you're busy. Why Sunday? you ask. Cause I didn't wanna go to church! I always figured that if I could convince my folks that going to church was going to get in the way of my schoolwork they would let me stay home, right? Wrong. Backfired on me every time.

My mom would come out doing that half stomp/

strut/jog she'd be doin' every Sunday mornin' trying to put her shoes and earrings on at the same time, and she'd say, "Hadjii, let's go." And she'd stop right in the middle of her sentence and say, "What are you doin'?" and I'd be like, "Mama, I can't go to church today." She'd say, "Oh really?" Not "Oh really," like, "Okay, well let's see if we can work it out." But "Oh really," like, "It's Sunday mornin', I'm late, I gotta stop and getcha grandmama a paper, and you wanna pull this crap. Yeah, I'm dyin' to hear this shit." And I'd say, "Yeah man, I got this book report due tomorrow and ya know, I know how y'all are about education and me doin' somethin' with my life, cause I'm tryin' to succeed ya know. The way I see it, if I make good grades in school, I can go to a good college. Get a good job. Maybe own my own business or somethin', make a bunch of money, and then you and Daddy can retire in the Bahamas or somethin', but it all starts now. So as much as I like going to church, I'm willin' to make that sacrifice and sit this week out and stay here wit' these borin'-ass books so I can make a better life for you and Father. After all you've done for me, it's the least I can do. It's my reasonable service. Tell Rev' and them I said hey."

Then my mom would just stare at me for a minute or two. Sizing me up like one of the showdowns in the westerns. And then she'd get real slick on me and say, "Fine." And I'd be thinking to myself, *You mean that shit actually worked? I won?* Then she'd say, "If it's okay witcha daddy." "!@$!*%!," I'd say.

Then I'd look up and there he was standin' in the

damn doorway again. What is it with him and doorways? By the way, did I mention that my dad had a terrible smoking problem? I think he started smoking cigarettes when he was like fourteen years old and never stopped and you could tell it had taken its toll on his lungs, cause he had this way of breathing that kinda sounded either like Darth Vader or one of those bad soap opera actors. So once you combined the breathing with the eyes and the height and the demeanor and his inability to smile, the nigga had what some people like to call *a presence* about himself. Not a Sean Connery presence. More like a *Friday the 13th* Jason-in-the-woods-type presence. But'chall know me. I ain't easily discouraged. I figure if you're down to ya last quarter might as well put it in the slot machine.

Then he'd say, "What's the problem?" and I'd be thinkin', *Damn, Daddy. Why does there always have to be a fuckin' problem? Why can't me and Mama ever just talk and work things out wit'out you sometimes?* Then I'd say, "Nothin'." Then my mom would say, "Your son" (often in moments like these she wouldn't claim me) "can't go to church today because he's got a book report due tomorrow." Then I'd say, "Damn, Mom, you just totally fucked up my pitch. You ain't mention college, the Bahamas, or none of that shit. Sometimes I feel like I'm just wastin' my breath around here. Anyway, yeah Daddy, it's actually bigger than a mere book report, or any report for that matter. It's actually a *project*, thus the need for all the encyclopedias, index cards, calculator, and so on and

so forth." (There's something about calculators and index cards that makes everything seem more professional.) "And ya know I gotta get all this information
together. Wait. Fuck that! I gotta compile *data*. Yep, this
ain't just regular information. This is *data*, nigga. I gotta
compile data, and get some stats together, and a graph
and shit. Not the bars, but the pie-lookin' one. Matter of
fact, I think I'm even gonna need a bibliography for this
one, cause this is some heavy shit. By the way, Mama, you
know you're gonna have to type all this up for me when
you get home from church tonight? Oh, and please bring
home a posterboard. Preferably *yellow*."

Then my dad would say, "It's due tomorrow?" And I'd
say, "Yep." "And you've known about this for how long?"
And I'd say, "Ohhhhh about a week or so, give or take a
month . . . or two." And he'd reply, "You've known
about this for two months and you've waited until the
day before it's due to start on it?" "Nah Daddy. I mean
that's how it may look, but technically I bought these index cards damn near three weeks ago." Then they'd both
say what every parent who actually cares about their
kid's life has said at least a thousand times. "How many
times have I told you about putting things off until the
last minute?" Then I'd say, "Ya know what, Daddy, maybe
if you didn't always wait until the last minute to remind
me that I shouldn't wait until the last minute I wouldn't
wait until the last minute all the time." And that, ladies
and gentlemen, is how I got this chipped tooth.

Anyway, like I said before, church wasn't so bad when

I was a kid because I could just sit there, play, eat candy, go to sleep, or whatever it took for my mom to keep me still. Then after the first song, this middle-aged black woman would stand up and turn around to the rest of the church, then all the kids would get up and follow her to "the back." For those of you who don't know, in the black church "the back" is some serious shit. No kid in their right mind wanted to go to the back, but as soon as that lady stood up they'd just all follow her back there like zombies.

I used to feel sorry for them niggas until one Sunday when we were sitting in church and the lady stood up and my mom nudged me like, "Go on back there." I was like, "Excuse me?" Then she replied, "You're of age now. Put those toys down and go to the back."

And I got up all slow as hell, like, "I can't believe this shit is happenin' to me. You know what they do to niggas in the back? The back is . . . the back is . . . the back is where they have *Sunday school*." And right then you know your life will never be the same again, cause once you hit Sunday school, you know Easter speeches, Christmas plays, hosting the spring pageant, fish fries, reading The Welcome, Bible study, choir practice, usher board meetings, junior usher board meetings, church anniversaries, pastor appreciation days, choir anniversaries, building fund-raisers, spring carnivals, summer picnics, fall banquets, winter prayer meetings, car washes, bake sales, vacation Bible school, and revivals are just around the corner. Heaven help me, I done fucked around and became a member of the church, and quite frankly, I've got toys to play with, comic books to read, and all kinds of other important stuff to do. Mama, I don't think I'm gonna be able to work the back into my schedule. But she wouldn't listen.

So you go in for your first day of Sunday school. The lady puts a workbook in front of you and boom. You've gotta jump right on in with everybody else. That's the thing about black churches, man. Ain't no feelin' ya out time. The Bible says we're supposed to plant the seed, but black folks be wantin' to put supergrow on ya. "Get saved today, little boy! That is unless you wanna go to a fiery hell! Ya know, just cause you're six years old don't mean you can't die in a car accident on the way home and find your little punk ass in hell!" Then five minutes later they're dousing you with water and the next thing ya know, you're on the usher board.

And the older you get the more aggressive people get about bringin' you over to King Jesus. Which doesn't bother me, but sometimes they can be a bit pushy. And they always catch me at the worst times, too. Like I'm in line at the movies and here comes one.

"Hey brotha! How ya doin'?"

And you're like, "I ain't got no change, man."

And they reply, "Nah, brotha, I don't wantcha change. I can make a withdrawal any time I want from the Greatest Banker the World's Ever Known. The Ultimate Provider."

"Oh well, that's good, man."

Then they ask, "Do you know Him?"

And I say, "Oh no. I don't have a bank account. I just keep all my money in my sock drawer next to my condoms."

"So you don't know Jesus?"

"Oh! Now I get it. I didn't know you were speakin' *Jesus* to me. I thought we were still talkin' about banks."

"So what are you here to see?"

"Who, me? I'm about to check out Tarantino's new movie, *Death, Vengeance, and Sluts.*

Then the witness shouts, "Hey y'all, we got one over here!" and the next thing ya know, twenty black people come grab you and throw you on the back of a church bus.

But my favorites are the white ones though, cause they're a little more creative. They have props and candy and those little green Bibles. They're sneaky too, cause sometimes they even wear costumes and they'll come up to ya in the mall dressed up like a pirate or somethin' and say, " 'Scuse me, mate, but I'ma searchin' for souls. Are ya lookin' for treasure? Arrgg!"

And I'm thinkin', *Oooh pirates are cool! Where's ya pot of gold? Or is that leprechauns? Or Smurfs? Or midgets?* Anyway, "Where's the treasure, Mr. Pirate?"

"Well you're not gonna find it in this here Victoria's Secret witcha girlfriend, mate. Arrrgg!" They got me again! But let's get back to church.

It's just in a kid's nature to not wanna join shit no matter how good it may be for them, but parents seem to disregard stuff like that. All that matters right now is the fact that they want'chou to join stuff, especially the youth choir. Your mom always has to force you to join the youth choir, which, I guess they mean well, but it always kinda frightens me when I see kids in the choir, cause you know up to sixty-five percent of the kids in the youth choir don't want to be up there. So it's like, you're making me fake it in front of God, cause I'd be up in the choir mad as hell. And my mom would say we're supposed to make a joyful noise unto the Lord, and I'm thinking, Yeah, but I can't even sing. Why can't we draw a picture or do something I'm good at?

See, my first church was a "chuch." One of them good ole, down-home, backwoods, dirt parking lot, wooden pews, with the wooden floors where the wood cracked up under ya feet when ya walked in, and ya got that good low bass when the old folks stomped on it while singing, with the little bathrooms on the side, and the kitchen with that supercold concrete floor, and had a cemetery in the back. That's what I'm talkin' 'bout! Old-school church. No air conditioning. Just those little fans the ushers would pass out with the pictures on 'em. One was a picture of Jesus praying, one was a picture of Jesus knocking on the door, another one was a picture of this black lady who I think was supposed to be Mahalia Jackson cause she was wearing a choir robe, and of course every brotha and sista out there knows ya had to have the one with Martin Luther King on it. I'm talkin' 'bout an old-school church. The ones where midway through the preacher's sermon half of the women would get up and go in the kitchen and start making dinner. Even the preacher used to be persuaded to end his sermon early once the aroma of that honey-baked ham started gettin' all up his nose.

But what really gave our church that down-home Southern flavor was, of course, the members. The people. The congregation. The body. Know why? Cause we had a church full of old folks. Those *authentic* old black people like the ones you see in the history books. See, old black people now are kind of polished. Some kids have grandparents who can still drive and have black hair and still dress nice and all that. Not my church. My church was full of some of the dustiest old folks you could find this side of slavery. I'm talkin' about those real old folks that couldn't stand up without a cane and five people helpin' 'em. Those old folks who always smelled like a mixture of mothballs, cologne, perfume, and butterscotch candy. We had those good old-school old folks that used to get up in the middle of church and say a bunch of nothin' and then burst into song like they were ordering food in a McDonald's commercial. And don't let it be one of those big sistas that could sing they asses off. They'd always sing a little bit and then the song would get too good for 'em and they say, "Ooh, sometimes thangs get so rough ya just gotta—" and then they'da start hummin' and moanin' and shit. It doesn't get any more down-home than that.

We also used to have those old windows that looked kind of like the glass door on your shower. That way you can't see what's going on outside and therefore you ain't got a clue of what time it is, cause church used to last all

day! Now mind you, I couldn't go outside after dark, yet
on Sunday we were in church till at least seven o'clock.
That's why I really hated church so much. Cause it was
cutting into my playtime. I could just feel my entire
Sunday slippin' away. Cause okay, in all honesty, we'd
probably get out of church around two or three, if we
were lucky. Ya know, that means if there wasn't no an-
niversary, or baptisms, baby dedications, or nothing like
that. Cause if it was one of those "special Sundays," oh,
believe me, we're gonna be there until Tuesday night!

But ya know you've really-really got a good down-
home church when you've got a good ole black preacher
who's about ninety-seven years old who week after week
gets up and preaches sermons that make absolutely no
fuckin' sense. And out of respect for "da chuch" and old
people we go along wit' that bullshit, but seriously,
would you respect anybody else who conducted business
in that manner? I mean, if you went to your kid's school
one day and saw your kid's math teacher standin' in front
of the class screamin', "Algebra! Ohhh Algebraaa!,"
you'd pull your kid outta that fuckin' class, wouldn't ya?
And I know a lot of you out there are thinking I shouldn't
be talkin' about the man of God like that, but come on
now. Do you honestly think God hired all of these cats?
I know the Lord works in mysterious ways, but somehow
I just can't imagine that God would look down from
heaven and say, "Hey, see the one with the Jheri curl and
the gold tooth wearin' the pink gators? . . . Let's give him
a job."

Now I always knew that after church we were still gonna end up spending another hour or two at my grandparents' house, which was gonna take us up to about four. Got a thirty-minute drive home. Four-thirty. I figured that if I played my cards right and changed clothes as quickly as possible, I could be on my bike by four-thirty-five and still squeeze me a couple of quality hours of playin' in before dark. That is, "If we leave now, Mama!" Because all week my mom's been talkin' trash about how she was gonna relax this Sunday. And I'd be like, "Hell yeah!" cause whenever she said she was gonna relax, that meant she was in a rush to get home so she could take a nap, which meant she wasn't gonna bother me, cause Sunday's like the only chance a family woman with young kids ever has at a nap. They work all week, and on Saturdays they're runnin' around helpin' everybody out, so on a Sunday when there isn't some special program, which is only like four times a year, Mom's relaxing and I'm playin'. If we could just get out of the fuckin' parking lot.

The walk through the parking lot to the car after church ain't never work out for me. You know how it is. After church, everybody kind of gathers outside for a little bit. Kids chase each other, men talk about last night's or today's game, advise each other on what type of fertilizer they need to put on their yard, and flirt with all the women. Women talk about diets and who's having surgery when, and old people threaten little kids. I don't know what the hell old people get out of threatening little kids, but I know it ain't that funny. It would always be some old dude sayin' somethin' like, "Ya know, you gettin' big, boy. Ya need to come over to my house so I can putcha to work," and old women were always askin' ya, "You wanna come home wit' me? You wanna stay at my house for a while? You wanna play wit' my grandbabies?" Then I'd reply, "Hell no! Now go on from 'round here wit' that bullshit. I'm trying to get home. Don't you see the sunlight's fadin'? I gotta go!"

Alright, so now we're doing good, right? We're almost to the car. My mom's brushed some people off in that nice church woman way. "Well alright. I'll talk to you later. Tell'em I said hey. See ya. Yeah gimme a call. Bless you, too." And you're almost to the car. And then it happens. Ya know how you have those times in your life where something bad happened, but it really could've been avoided fairly easily if you would've done just one thing differently? Check this one out and tell me if it sounds familiar. We're finally in the car and we're ready to leave. Mom's in the driver seat. You're on the passenger side. She's going through her purse looking for her keys, trying to find her glasses, etc., and then one of your cousins or best friends comes over to your door and says, "Ay, you'll roll the window down for a minute? Lemme ask ya somethin'." So you roll the window down and he says, "Ay, I just wanted to say—" and then they punch you in the arm and take off runnin'. Oh hell nah! It's the Last Lick Game. I know this nigga ain't tryin' to get last lick on me? Now I've got a vital decision to make. Do I (*a*) listen to my mama and keep my black behind in this car? Or do I (*b*) piss my mama off by jumpin' outta this car and tryin' to chase this nigga down even though I know I have absolutely no chance of catching him? Aww hell, I got my pride. "Come'ere, boy!"

So you jump out of the car and by some stroke of luck, you finally do catch up with him and you hit him, then he hits you, then you hit him, then he hits you, then y'all grab each other by the shirttails, and you're both hitting each other simultaneously. Then you hear your mom screamin' from the car, "Boy, get back in this car!" Then your rival screams, "Yeah, you heard ya mama! Go get in the car!" Then he makes a spin move on you that frees his shirt from your grip, and he gets the last lick before runnin' off into the sunset.

All this takes place in a matter of only about three minutes, but you're soon to find out that that was too long, because now as you're returning to the car you see that some black woman with one of them double names like Susie Mae or Kathy Cathy has your mama hemmed up now and is talkin' her back out. Cause Susie Mae's a God-fearin' woman, and she's a good woman too. Ya know how old women get when they get, well, old, and the Lord Jesus Christ not only becomes their Lord and Savior, but He's their provider, adviser, doctor, confidant, and boyfriend too? Ya ask'em, "We're havin' dinner tonight. Would you like to come and join us?" and they say, "No. I think me and Jesus plan on stayin' in tonight." You know you're gettin' old when the highlight of your week becomes the Friday night game of Battleship that you've scheduled with Jesus. You know you're getting even older when Jesus says, "Not tonight. I've got a headache."

Anyway, Susie Mae was one of the sweetest ladies you'll ever meet, but bless her heart, her problem was she was one of the most depressing people in the world. You know how there's always that one older black woman in your family, on your job, in your church, whose entire life has been full of pain? That's Susie Mae. Now as sorry as I felt for her, I still wanted my mom to tell her to shut the hell up so we could go, but she never did. But on the real, it didn't even matter anymore that I wasn't going to make it home in time to play, because after a good sit-down with Susie Mae and hearin' all the things that she was going through, I knew I'd never complain about shit like missing out on my whole Sunday again because I realized that I had a wonderful life compared to Susie Mae's.

SUSIE MAE: Hey Sista Hand. How you doin'?

MOM: I'm fine. How 'bout you?

SUSIE MAE: Child, I'm just holdin' on to God's
  unchangin' hand.

ME: (thinking) *Yeah, you and everybody else. Who
  gives a shit? Yo Mama, tell this lady we gotta go. I
  got playin' to do. And don't go askin' her no
  bullshit about her life. I said, don't ask her . . .
  don't ask'er . . . don't ask'er!*

MOM: So, how have things been?

ME: *DAMN IT, MAMA!*

SUSIE MAE: Oh, I don't really wanna talk about it right now. I know you tryin' to get home and take care of ya family. I'll be alright.

MOM: Okay then, well, call me and I'll—

SUSIE MAE: It's just that it seems like the devil won't let up on me. Lately I been gettin' this pain that start up in my throat and then shoots down around to my elbow, then back up to my shoulder, and it's drivin' me crazy. Doctor say he think it's stress, but I think I need to get a second opinion, cause ya know my arthritis been flarin' up lately. Other mornin' it took me three hours to get out of the bed. Plus once I did get out, my foot had swole up to the size of a melon. Not a watermelon, but one of them honeydew melons. Couldn't even put my shoe on so I had to go to work barefooted on the one side. Ended up havin' to walk five miles to work, cause none of my kids would give me a ride. Then I got fired cause I showed up for work three hours late and barefooted on the one side and you can't be workin' in nobody's kitchen when you're barefooted on the one side, so now I done lost my job. Which means now I ain't got no health insurance, which is unfortunate cause I stepped on a heroin needle when I was walkin' to the unemployment office. Doctor say it's gonna have to get amputated, but I can't afford to get it amputated so I'm just gonna pray about it and let God's will be done. Umm-hmm.

And I used to feel so sorry for Susie Mae cause even her good news was shitty. Because good women with those big ole hearts always seemed to be surrounded by some of the biggest assholes in the world. But they never lose their faith.

> SUSIE MAE: (continues) But other than that I'm doin' alright. My oldest son James just got married, ya know?
> MOM: Oh really? That's wonderful!
> SUSIE MAE: Umm-hmm. Married a real pretty girl too. Or at least that's what they tell me. Ya know I wasn't invited to the wedding. I've never even met'er ya see, cause once I finished payin' for my oldest son's college education he told me I couldn't ever come visit him at his house cause ya know I was workin' two jobs? One down to the meat market cuttin' raw meat, and in the nighttime I'd go down to clean up at the school. Then on the weekends I head shrimp down to the dock so I ain't never been known to smell too good, and I guess he didn't want me comin' up there makin'em look bad, and I guess he was right cause now he's a big-time doctor makin' a lot of money, but now that I ain't got no job and no insurance I can't afford'em no mo'. But he did give me a loan with a reasonable interest rate. I just thank God that he ain't forgot where he came from.
> MOM: I thought you were workin' at the mill?

SUSIE MAE: I was, but after years of inhalin' all
them fumes off the chemicals, doctor say my lungs
is all shriveled up. Which is why I can't be around
no cigarette smoke or else I'll die right there on the
spot, and ya know my husband smoke them
cigarettes, and you know it's hard to quit so he left
me and moved in wit' my sister cause she don't
mind cigarette smoke. Last I heard they was doin'
real good and she was expectin' a boy, which is
kinda confusin' to me cause I don't know if he's
supposed to be my nephew or my stepson? But in
all things give thanks. I'm just happy to be alive.
Every day is a blessin'. Just the other day I was
thinkin' about how lucky I am to be here, cause
after them police officers kicked in my door and
beat me into a coma that time over some kilos of
cocaine my grandson had left in my attic, I know,
"That ain't nothin' but God's grace."

I tried everything to get out of church, from school
projects to sickness to trying to convince my mom that I
was possessed by demons and I didn't wanna go to
church and get no demons on anybody, but none of it
ever worked. And since I was always at church, that
meant that every year I had to be in the got damn Easter
play.

Now Easter's very important, because I really do believe that Jesus died for our sins and that's a pretty big
deal that should be celebrated. The only thing about

Easter is, it's too damn stressful. At least in the black community. I'm a grown man and I'm still experiencing some trauma suffered during Easters from my childhood.

Cause I grew up in "da chuch," and in da chuch Easter Sunday is like the Superbowl. Except instead of coaches tellin' you what to do, you've got big fat black women who love the Lord, live for Easter, and don't take no shit off no kids. And instead of a football game, we've gotta be in the Easter play. Can you say pressure cooker? During rehearsals you'd go backstage and see a bunch of nine-year-olds smoking cigarettes, trying to hold it together. That's what Easter's like in da chuch.

See, every church has the Christmas play, but that one's easy. Three dudes, Mary, a baby Jesus, a few goats, and call it a day. Plus nobody ever performs the Christmas play on the actual day of Christmas, so it's more laid-back, but the Easter play actually goes down on Easter Sunday, and everybody, and I mean evvvvery-body, comes to church on Easter Sunday. People who don't ever come to church none of the other fifty-one Sundays of the year come on Easter. Winos come to church on Easter. Even daddies (except for mine) come to church on Easter. Even the baby-daddies come to church on Easter. I know some cats that end up havin' to hit like four, five different Easter shows all over town just to see all their kids perform. So the house is gonna be packed!

So with that in mind you have to understand that Easter is like a Black Woman's Showcase. First you've got the director of the play. Usually one of two types of sisters in the church want to direct the play. There's the young sister who's really having a hard time with the whole Christian lifestyle thing, cause she's got that young-quiet-sexy thing goin' on. Ya know that cute, supernice girl in your church that always makes terrible choices in men? So every time she tries to sing a solo in church she can't ever make it through the song without breakin' down cause the lyrics of the song remind her of some dude that's been breakin' her heart week after week. She's one of them. But she earns her keep in the church because she always love to work with the kids.

Now on the other hand you've got Sista Patti or Sista Cathy who take these performances just a tad too seriously. Sista Cathy's one of those black women who doesn't play when it comes to the Lord's work! You know those women in the church with the big ole booties that get a kick out of tellin' little kids off? Like you might be in church and see two kids sitting with their mother and then she'll go to the bathroom and leave the kids on the pew. This is usually when one of the kids uses this moment of freedom as an opportunity to slap their brother or somethin'. Sista Cathy'll turn around and yell at kids she doesn't even know. One of those women that'll make ya spit ya gum out into her bare hand, no napkin, no nothin'. You know, one of those black women who have been going to the church so long that they've given themselves their own title? Somethin' crazy like Sista Deaconess Heir to the Elders of the Church First Lady Madam?

So you pray and pray that the young chick gets to direct the Easter play, because she's nice and she's usually pretty so you've got a crush on her, but Sista Cathy ends up directing the Easter play anyway.

Now there are two types of Easter plays. There are the ones that are your standard, typical "Easter plays," and then there are the ones where Sista Cathy decides she wants to *get her playwright on.* Remember how we said a little earlier that whenever someone says, "We need to talk," something bad's on the way? It's kind of like that. Cause the last thing a room full of kids wants to hear is a grown woman in her mid-fifties say, "We're gonna try something new this year." Watch out!

First things first. We've got to assign parts. Which is really BS, cause you know how it is. Every year everybody gets the same parts. The older kids get to set up the stage. The old kid who isn't quite old enough to be on the stage crew, but's still too old to be in the Kiddie Easter play (mothers can be some cruel individuals, boy), gets the part with all the big words. That's usually the narrator. The smart kid always gets the part with the most shit to remember. The short-bus kid gets one or two lines. Usually something short and sweet like, "Where the eggs?," and the cute girl with the pretty hair always opens and closes the show. That's how it goes. Dumb kids try to get promoted every year, but to no avail.

But that's only the beginning, because everybody knows Easter's all about the real woman, or should I say the First Lady, in your life. Your mom. The show's all about Mama. And I'm sure it's the same for white people or whoever else. Maybe not. But black people have a fascination with who's whose kid. "Oh, that's Susie's boy!" "That's Helen's daughter!" That's serious business because parents tend to identify themselves by how wonderful or fucked up their kid is. So it's either like a badge of honor or a one-way ticket to lifelong embarrassment. So the last thing you wanna do as a kid, and I mean the laaaaast thing you wanna do as a kid, is fuck up in the Easter play, cause your mom will never forgive you. My mom was a pretty pleasant woman the rest of the year, but boy, around Easter she'd flip her shit. I'm talkin' split personalities. I'd be in my room playin' with my toys and she'd kick in my door LAPD-style and start pacing back and forth in front of me and say some something like,

MOM: Now you listen and you listen good. Sunday is showtime. And instead of you bein' in here, practicin', and tryin' to hone your craft, (sinister) you in here playin' wit' those stupid toys. But I swear on my own grave—hold up, (definite) I swear on *your* grave—that come Sunday, you ain't gon' embarrass me. Not on my watch. Look at me! (stumbling) Wh-wh-whe-where's ya script at, boy? Have you memorized your lines yet?

ME: No ma'am.

MOM: Oh, so you just *want* to go to hell, dontcha? Well don't let me stand in your way.

ME: Okay.

MOM: Boy, getcha script out and let's practice. Now say it!

ME: My name is Hadjii

and I'm here to say
Happy-Happy Easter Day

MOM: Again.

ME: My name is Hadjii—

MOM: Hoogie? Hoggy? I can barely understand a
word you're sayin'. Enunciate!

ME: My name is Haaaaadddjjjiiiiii and I'm—

MOM: Oh, you got jokes now? You tryin' to be
funny?

ME: (whining) Noooo maaannnn shoooot.

Note: *Man shoot*, translated from child terminology,
means, "I'm tired of this shit. Leave me the fuck alone,
got damn it!" Little did I know my mom spoke "Child."

MOM: What did you say?

ME: I said ha-choo, I'm sneezin'. *Ha-choo, ha-choo.*

MOM: Now you listen here. Saturday mornin' we're
gonna get up and I'm droppin' you off at the
barbershop and you gonna get'cho hair cut while
me and ya grandmama go shoppin'. Then ya goin'
to ya last rehearsal. After that we goin' to Sears,
cause you're wearin' a suit this year. Now come
Sunday you better speak clearly—

Ya ever notice how clearly people say *clearly* when
they want you to speak clearly?

MOM: You better speak cleaaarrrllly and you better
project. I wanna be able to hear you all the way in

the back! Okay? Now take ya behind outside and
practice your lines. I'm gonna be in the kitchen
with the window open so I can hear you. I'll
let'chou back in when I'm satisfied.

And I'd go outside thinking to myself, *Damn, why is
she trippin'? I've only got three lines. My name is Hadjii,
blah-blah-blah, Happy Easter, got damn it. What the
fuck? I ain't gotta practice that shit. I'm nine years old.
I've been the ring bearer in three weddings and read the
lunch menu over the intercom at school. I'm a pro at this
kind of shit.*
Then the big day comes and it's your time to shine and
make your mama proud, and you go up there in front of
a church filled with people and say . . .

ME: My name is . . . My name is . . . uhh . . . uhh . . .
Aww, fuck me! My name is . . . (thinking) *Aww
hell, I done fucked up on my method acting. Come
on, Hadjii. What is your name?*

Then all the sudden, you look up and see your mom
on her knees in front of the front row doing that loud
whisper mothers do when they're pissed off.

MOM: (whispering) Hadjii! Your name is HADJII!
ME: (crying) My name is Hadjii
And I'd like to say . . .
Happy Saint Patrick's Day?

to where they weren't facing the other nine kids, like turn their back on them, and then throw the ball over their shoulder to the rest of us and whoever caught it would then try to run and score. Hotball has got to be one of the number one killers of black youth in America. And there was always one kid who was too damn old to be playin' with kids our age. He was a killer, and nobody could ever tackle'em, butcha had to try cause ya gotta get your stripes. So when the older kids came and wanted to play, you just had to grin and bear it and try not to get your head knocked off.

It was tough being a kid. Especially when you're little, cause the older kids were always fuckin' with you. We're tryin' to play basketball, and here they come, takin' over the court. Takin' your basketball, especially the old-old cats that were like twenty-five and shit but still lived with their mama and rode bicycles around the neighborhood. They'd be at the park getting drunk and high and then wanna "borrow" your basketball. I hated them niggas. But then on the other hand, you couldn't wait to grow up so you could become one of 'em and terrorize some little kids too. And they used to always wanna take your bike to the store. That's where I drew the line. I knew I might get cursed out, maybe even roughed up a little bit, but it ain't matter, cause you weren't getting my bike. Know why? Cause as scared as I was of those dudes, I was waaaay more afraid of my daddy. And do you know what woulda happened if my pops would've come outside and saw some stranger riding my bike? The bike they just got me for Christmas? Sorry, buddy, but you're gonna have to kill me in order to take my bike to the store. Plus I had to be in by dark, which during the winter meant five-thirty, and I didn't get home from school until like four, so if I let a kid take my bike, they might not come back with it until like seven-thirty. Then I either had to come home late and act like I was just hard-core disrespecting the curfew (cause I couldn't tell'em I was late because somebody had my bike) or I ran the risk of the worst shit in the world: my mom coming to get me.

When that happened, it would be just like in the movies right before a drive-by. I would be out playing and then all the sudden it's like you can hear a silence. Then you'd look up and see a car slowly coming to a halt about five houses down. All the kids would be like, "Whose mom is that?" "Ain't mine. My mama dead." "Ain't mine. We ain't got no car." "Hadjii, is that yo mama? Hadjii? Where did he go?" I was waaay down the street by the time they even noticed I was gone, cause I could run fast as hell when I thought I was in trouble. All black kids can. That's why the police don't even bother chasing us. It's pointless, cause you ain't gonna catch no scared kid. That's just a rite of passage. By the time we were ten years old, we were some fast-runnin' fence-jumpin' muthafuckas. Learned how to do that runnin' from them crazy dogs all the time. I'd be runnin' so fast it could be raining and I wouldn't even get wet. Cause for some dumb reason I always thought that as long as I beat her home, it wasn't really like I broke curfew. Wrong. Now I'm on punishment.

I hated punishment. As much as I hated ass whuppins, at least they were quick. Punishment would last for
like a week. The worse the crime, the longer the time.
Breaking curfew was like a three to five. Days, that is. A
bad report card was like a week or two, but couldn't
nothin' compare wit' a teacher calling home. I wasn't
ever any big type of troublemaker or nothin', but ya
know, I could be silly at times. Small-scale class clown
and teachers would call home and lie, yes lie, about how
I was disrupting class, like "Yeah, Mrs. Hand, this is Mrs.
Collins, Hadjii's math teacher. I'm sorry to bother you
this evening, but Hadjii seems to have a problem with
talking during class. I've tried to address this issue with
him several times, but he told me to go and fuck myself.
Yes, umm-hmm, real tough guy. Smokes weed in class
and everything." And my mom would be like, "Oh
really? Well, thank you for making me aware of this.
Please feel free to call me anytime and keep me abreast
on these developments as they take place." And I'd be on
the sofa watching TV thinkin' to myself, "Did my mama
just say *abreast*? Got damn it. Another teacher done
called." Then my mom would tell the teacher, "Me and
his father will most definitely handle that. Matter of fact,
here's my work number. Next time he gets outta line I'll
be more than happy to come up there on my lunch break
and straighten him out for you."

"Mrs. Hand, I don't think violence is the answer."

"And you're entitled to your opinion, Mrs. Collins,
but it's on and poppin' now. So like I said. Call me."

The next day I'd show up at school with a walker.

"Oh Hadjii, what happened?" Mrs. Collins would ask. "Bitch, you know what happened! You coulda made me clean the chalkboard or made me write some shit a hundred times, but nooooooooo, you wanna call a nigga parents. Well, I hope you're satisfied. Now I got a lazy eye cause of you."

But times weren't always bad. Most of the time they were great, cause like I said, we knew how to play . . . And the best thing in the world was when one of my cousins got to spend the night over at my crib. Not even the rain could stop us from havin' a good time, cause we'd just make up games. Looking back on it, there's probably nothing more frightening than two little boys making up shit to do. I mean, we had our more innocent games too. Like, strikeout was where me and my cousin would pitch a tennis ball to each other (again, nobody was stupid enough to give us a baseball; giving kids a baseball is like giving a crack addict your wallet) and try to strike each other out. But the majority of our games were those crazy-ass, gotta-hurt-yaself games that were usually inspired by movies and television. Like Rocky, for example. We'd put socks on our hands to pose as boxing gloves, take our shirts off, and then literally beat the shit outta each other. You know how many teeth I lost playin' Rocky? A small amount in comparison to our other game, karate fight. We went and saw *Karate Kid* at the movies and my cousin was like, "We got a new game!" We'd stand in the living room and fight each other karate-style. That bastard used to knock one of my

teeth out nearly every week. Probably why I got this dis-
position now. I sucked at karate fight. But I got'em back
when we got a little older, cause that's when we started
playin' match fight. Match fight is when the both of
you have a pack of matches and strike one and then try
to throw it at your opponent. I was a match-throwin'
muthafucka. I could throw a match ten feet without it
goin' out. It's all in the wrist. I threw matches so good I
even caught the curtains on fire once, and that's when my
parents made me retire from my match-fighting career.
Wasn't an honorable ceremony either. So then of course,
once you're tired of getting your ass kicked in Rocky and
karate fight, and your parents have threatened to send
you to a shelter if they ever catch you playin' with
matches again, what's the only thing left for a kid to do?
Flip on the bed! We were some bed-flippin' fanatics!
Gettin' you a nice runnin' start and flippin' onto a bed
was better than sex to us. Cause we ain't know what sex
was yet. But to this day, whenever I'm in one of those
nice hotels with the quality cushioned beds, I still bust a
flip on it. Can't help it. Let that be a lesson to all you
youngsters out there. If you ever find yourself in a hotel
room with a lovely young lady and you really wanna turn
her on, flip on the bed for her. Drives'em wild.

Only thing is, when you're young, you don't realize
the difference between quality beds and your bed. For example, the beds in a hotel are usually pretty sturdy beds.
However, the bed in the guest room of your house probably isn't of the highest quality. That's why it's in the

fuckin' guest room. But you don't know that. It's not like you can go and ask your mom if this bed is flipworthy. You just gotta test it out for yourself. That's when you get up on the bed and jump up and down a couple of times and then try to nail a perfectly executed Greg Louganis triple somersault on it. Then you land on the mattress and hear that *bing.* You know that *bing.* That's the *bing* ya hear when you're a kid everytime you break some shit with some iron in it. See, there's *smash* for smaller offenses like knocking over a lamp with a basketball while trying to hone your dribbling skills. Then there's *crack* for when ya break wooden stuff like when you get body-slammed on the "good sofa" and you completely tear up the entire base of it. And last but not least, there's *bing.* Whenever you heard *bing* you knew that you just broke some shit that you couldn't fix by yourself. Damn it. If Pops sees this he's gonna flip his shit.

The only time you can tell ya daddy you broke something in the house is if it was some shit that he hated too, like the family picture, or if y'all broke something together tryin' to do some manly shit, cause daddies break stuff around the house all the time. Way more stuff than kids'll ever break. And not only do they break more stuff, but they break all the important shit. Like the stove, the air conditioner, the TV. It always goes down the same way. Something in the house isn't quite broken, but it just isn't working as well as it's supposed to. Then your pops gets the bright idea to try and fix it himself. Now your mom, being the wise one, says, "Oh, the toilet's not working properly? I'll get the plumber to come take a look at it this week." Then your dad says, "Fuck a plumber. We ain't got no money to be payin' no plumber for something we can fix ourselves. Lemme take a look at it." Then Pops would pull out the duct tape. Duct tape was his answer to everything. Pipe's leaking? "Bring me the duct tape." TV's messed up? "Hold that antenna in position and lemme duct-tape that sucka down." Duct tape on the remote control. Got dishes duct-taped together. Mama's got a run in her stockings. He tryin' to duct-tape that shit. "Hadjii broke his arm? Duct tape, please." Now it wasn't a big deal to me, but my mom used to get pissed the fuck off, cause women who work hard to keep the house clean and want everything in the right order in case company ever comes over can't stand a duct-taping-ass man. How does it look if you have some guests come over and you got the chandelier duct-taped to the ceiling?

And whenever the duct tape didn't work, Pops would just go to plan B: just hit it. Just bang on it till it gets in line. It works on Hadjii. However, appliances don't necessarily respond in the same manner. Something might happen to the TV like the volume isn't sounding quite as loud to Daddy as it used to, possibly because he's got Miles Davis blasting in the background. So first he'd try to duct-tape the speaker, then if that didn't work, he'd just bang on it. Now we've only got a two-inch picture screen. Thanks a lot, Dad. Watching TV shows and only seeing everybody's belly button is fuckin' neato.

But as much as he loved duct tape and banging on shit, he never thought it was quite as amusing when I tried to fix some shit without his approval. The worst was when I would be in my room or wherever in the house and I broke some shit and it made that loud *bang* that they could hear in the living room. It didn't even give you time to come up with a good excuse. Like the time I broke the shower rod trying to do pull-ups on it. I mean damn, I was trying to get ready for karate fight. And parents can be real cold too, cause even if you hurt yourself they don't give a fuck. Cause by some strange stroke of luck, your parents have warned you about the dangers of every dumbass thing, stunt, or idea you'll ever wanna do in life before you ever even do it. So when you do it anyway and hurt the hell outta yaself, they feel like you deserved it. I remember my mom used to tell me, "Hadjii, stay away from that stove. Boy, I said don't go near the stove." Of course, being the rambunctious young man I was, and that all kids are, somebody tellin' you not to go near the stove only makes you wanna go near the stove that much more. And that's when your dad kicks in with that manly shit, like "Fuck it. Let'em learn the hard way. Go on in there and burn ya little ass up. Let that stove show you who's boss." I went over there, and y'all gotta keep in mind, this is an old-school stove. Nowadays you can leave an oven mitt on top of a hot stove and it won't even get hot, but back then you couldn't even walk by a stove without sweating, or maybe that was just our stove. Anyway, I felt like my existence would be meaningless if

I didn't walk by that stove, so I walked by the stove with no shirt on, and burnt the shit out of myself. Got the scar to prove it.

And ya know what? At first, getting hurt in that type of situation isn't that bad. I mean it's bad, but it ain't that bad. Cause at first your mom's like, "I told ya to stay away from that stove. That's whatcha get!" Which sounds bad, but I'll take that any day over what usually happens next. Cause now your mom wants to know *why*. *Why'd* you do it? *Why* were you flippin' on the bed? *Why* did you drill those holes in the coffee table? Why? Just tell me why! Women always wanna know why. And hey, I love the ladies. I believe in a woman's right to know. Just one problem. I don't know why. Seriously. I don't. See, moms all over the world don't understand this, but "I don't know" is a real answer to a kid. "Why were you throwing firecrackers at the dog?" I don't know. Seemed like a good idea at the time. We were having fun. I don't know. And for all you moms out there raising little boys and you wanna know why they do ninety-five percent of all the dumb shit they do. You wanna know why they stuck the fork in the socket? Why they put the goldfish in the microwave? Why they spray-painted their shoes? Blah-blah-blah. I'm gonna tell ya right now, when you ask them why, they're gonna say, "I don't know." Doesn't mean they're being disrespectful. Doesn't mean they're bad kids. Doesn't mean they're on their way to a life of crime either. Because translated in "boy" terms, "I don't know" means "I just wanted to see what would happen." Now of course you can never tell your mom that, but that's the truth. You just wanted to see what would happen. Little boys are the most curious muthafuckas on the face of the earth. That's why I can relate to mothers everywhere, cause I always wanted to know why too. It's just that they wanna know why you did it, and I wanted to know why *can't* I do it? . . . See, tellin' a kid not to do something isn't good enough. A kid's gotta know why. And it really doesn't matter what you say, a boy has to experience "why" for himself cause we're curious like that. And there is no limit to how far we'll go or what we'll try to satisfy our curiosity.

Like you know how a spray can of deodorant says "flammable"? Well, did you know that if you hold a spray can of deodorant up to an open flame and spray it, you've got a blow torch? Know how I know? Cause I tried it. And did you know that if you soak one of your action figures in rubbing alcohol and then light it on fire it'll catch fire without really burning your toy? Butcha gotta blow it out fast or else you'll turn your toy black. Know how I know that? Cause I tried it. And did you know that no matter how deep of a hole you dig, you can't dig all the way to hell, or China? Trust me. I tried it. Spent three days working on that hole. Now, had I actually reached hell, or China for that matter, I don't know what my next move would've been. Didn't plan that far ahead. I imagine the devil would've said, "Why in the fuck did you put a hole in my ceiling?" and I would've said, "I don't know." Then he would've replied, "Just wanted to see what would happen, huh? You know you get that from me, right? Should've drank more castor oil."

But as frustrating as the whole "why" ordeal can be, it ain't got nothing on step three of the injury process. Cause after your mom screams at you for being so stupid, and finally gets a "why" answer that's of satisfaction, her maternal and sensitive side kicks in. Now she wants to "help." Which usually meant waaay more pain than I was already experiencing was on the way. Like you know how you might be fuckin' around outside trying to jump ramps on ya bike and then ya fall in the street and scrape your knees to shreds? Then you run in the house kneeling over with your hands over your knees, crying and shit. Instantly your mom thinks it's something major, so she's like, "What happened?!" And you groan out some incomprehensible shit. So then she gets mad, "Lemme see it!" and you move your hands and your knees are covered in blood and now she's really mad, cause the average woman doesn't like blood too tight. Especially blood on the furniture. So she's like, "Sit still, boy!" But then the maternal side kicks in, and after she gets you to calm down and the crying's turned into hard breathing, and you're a little more relaxed now, she blows on it and says, "It's okay. Lemme clean that up for you." And you get excited cause you're thinkin', "Hell yeah, I'm finna get me a Band-Aid in this bitch!" cause kids love wearin' Band-Aids. That's damn near up there with a cast!

So your mom leaves the room and then comes back with some supplies. The first time something like this happened I rolled with it. I mean after all, this is my mom. She said she was gonna clean it up. I trust her. She'd never do anything to hurt me. Okay, so I see some Band-Aids. Good. A couple of gauzes. Okay. Some cotton balls. Interesting. Hmm. "Whatcha gonna do wit' that bottle of water, Mama? Oh, that ain't water? It's alcohol? What's alcohol? Oh. So you gonna put some alcohol on this knee to prevent infection? Sounds good. Hook it up, Mama. OWWWW BITCH! What the fuck is your problem?!" Alcohol on an open wound burns like hell! That shit stings so bad it almost makes you curse at your own mother! (Like I did a few lines up . . . in my mind.) After that first time, I vowed my mother would never "alcohol" me again. I'd be sitting on the toilet while my mom went through the medicine cabinet. She'd pull out that bottle of alcohol and I'd be like, "Woman, if you don't back the fuck up I swear I'ma—DAMN IT, MAMA! LISTEN TO ME!" Then she stepped it up a notch when she started buying this shit called Methalaid, Metholylaid, Methiolaid? Merthiolate! That's it! Merthiolate. I hated that crap! I mean, anytime a medication or drug starts with *meth*, or *mirth*, or *meph*, or any of that shit. That's a dead giveaway right there. Alcohol ain't have nothing on this stuff. It was like alcohol on steroids. First of all, it's a spray. I got a big open wound on my knee and you wanna spray it? On top of that, it was orange! You ain't supposed to put no orange shit on ya body!

Mothers are always abusing their kids in the name of

helping. Like when you're young and fall down in the parking lot or anywhere in public and you get your clothes dusty. Then your mom gets pissed because number one, you're "dirtyin' up your good clothes," and number two, everybody's looking at y'all now. So your mom can't hit'chou like she really wants to, so she *brushes* the dirt off. Funny, but brushing the dirt off always felt like gettin' slapped to me. I'd be thinking, "You're not brushing the dirt off. You're hitting me! I'm getting abused in front of everyone and they don't even realize it!"

Now in hindsight I know she really meant well ninety-nine percent of the time, but her helping just hurt too much. Like we'd be getting ready for church and I had like a little mini-Afro. Like not quite an Afro, but too much hair for a brush to be effective. So my mom would tell me, "Hadjii, go wash ya face and get dressed. And comb your hair!" Then she'd go in her bedroom and start getting dressed and we wouldn't see each other again until it was time to get in the car. So it's not like she's looking over my shoulder making sure I'm combing my hair, right? That's when I'd go in the bathroom and try to find the right comb. Cause I hadn't combed my hair all week, so it always took me a while to find *the right* comb. See, there were two types of combs. The big one and the little one. The big one was, well, big, but the little one was a bitch cause it had the two options on it. Like the teeth on the comb were real close together on one half. Then on the other side, the teeth were even closer together! Now you know this is the comb you're supposed to use, but you also know this is gonna hurt. But I'd try to comb it and I'd be off to a pretty rough start. Then the comb would get caught on one of those mean-ass thug naps that would make your whole head cock back and I'd be like, "Okay, there's gotta be a better way to go about this. I got it! I need some lubrication." So I opened up the medicine cabinet, but I didn't see anything. So then I looked under the sink. Now everybody knows ya mom keeps all the fucked-up shit under the sink with the cleaning products. And keep in mind, we're talking about under the sink in the guest bathroom. So that's the super-old shit nobody ever uses anymore, like an old dried-up sponge, one of them old scrub brushes to clean the toilet that's been sitting in there so long it's become rusty, an old container of baking soda, and eleven bottles of Old Spice and Brut from Christmases gone by. Then ya got some more stuff under there that company left behind from the time they stayed the night a couple of years ago. Like some old Q-tips, a couple of old toothbrushes, a half-used minibottle of mouthwash, some peroxide, some tampons, and lo and behold, guess what I found right next to the Drāno? Some muthafuckin' Pink Lotion!

Oh! I took y'all back on that one. What'chall know about that Pink Lotion? For all of my urbanly challenged out there, Pink Lotion is like a hair grease that comes in this pink-and-black bottle with a white top and you use it on ya hair to give it that shine, ya know. Man, I remember the first time I ran across a bottle of Pink Lotion. I

was about to go outside and play and I thought the shit
was real lotion. Ya know, like body lotion? I put that junk
on, and first of all, it took me like three hours to rub that
shit into my skin, but then once I got outside, I started
cookin'. Ya know how they've got Malibu Barbie? I was
Rotisserie Hadjii. Other kids was like, "Damn, Hadjii.
Why you sizzlin'?" Dogs kept lickin' my legs and shit. It
was awful. But anywho, I put half a bottle of Pink Lotion
in my hair, right? And it really made combing easier. I
started thinking to myself, "Ya know, . . . this ain't so
bad? Maybe I should comb my hair more often?" Then
ya get cocky and start combing it fast like you've got
"good hair." Which, by the way, you always hear black
people going back and forth about this whole good
hair/bad hair thing. And some people even go as far as to
say, "There's no such thing as good or bad hair. All hair's
good! When you call straight and curly hair 'good' you're
supporting European ideals." And to that I say, "Shut the
hell up." Maybe there's no such thing as good hair, but
bad hair is a very harsh reality that some of us less fortunate folks have to face, and I was a kid with bad hair.
And it was fucked up too, because when I was born
everybody thought I had a shot at being one of the priv-
ileged ones. If you were to see some of my baby pictures
you'd understand everyone's optimism. My hair was all
curly and soft. Everybody thought I had a future. But
once I turned four or so, my hair napped up like a muthafucka. My mom almost went into that postpartum de-
pression shit. Y'all don't know what I went through!

So I'm doing okay for a minute, but then I ran out of Pink Lotion and I've still got three-fourths of my hair left! So I'm just gonna have to man up and suffer through it. But eventually after gettin' hung up on a couple of those thug naps—ya know the ones on the back of ya neck? those real militant ones that won't budge for anybody?—I just kinda gave up on combing my hair and started trying to find a pick, right? Cause picks didn't hurt as bad, but I didn't have an Afro. I had a mini-'Fro. If you picked it, the top was gonna be all high and straight, but I ain't have enough hair for a pick to work on the sides, so I had to comb it. Then I remembered some words of wisdom I had gotten from my cousin once. He said, "Ya know, if ya wet'cha hair before ya comb it, it doesn't hurt as much." Sounded like a plan to me. So I drenched my hair to get it nice and soft and I must admit, he was on to something. That comb was rolling through my soft and smooth silky hair like a hot knife through butter, playa. Even on the sides! I'm lookin' good. All this good hair. I was feeling like one of them Sammy Davis Jr.–type niggas.

Then my mom would come out of her room, walking through the house with that frantic fast-paced walk that all women do when they're running late. Cause women get reeeeal testy when they're runnin' late. Again, my mom was a pretty pleasant woman most of the time, but when she was runnin' late for church she could say some real cruel shit to ya. You'd be like, "Mama, can we get an ice cream sundae after church?" And she'd snap like, "Ya know sometimes I wish you never born! Now help me put this bracelet on." Yes ma'am.

So between her trying to get dressed and checking to make sure the food wasn't gonna overcook (My mom would let shit cook all day on Sunday. We'd come home and the entire house would smell like pot roast. Now that's impressive! Cookin' shit while you ain't even home.), my mom was too busy to give me a proper inspection. She had too much on her plate. She'd be rushing so bad that every Sunday like clockwork we'd get in the car, drive halfway down the street, and then stop. She forgot her purse. Never failed. So now we've gotta turn around and go back. I'd always use this as an opportunity to say some smart shit she'd say to me in a situation like this, like, "See what happens when we're rushing and not taking our time?" Well, there goes my shot at that ice cream sundae after church, but I couldn't help myself.

Then we'd have to stop at the gas station to pick up the Sunday paper. Two copies. One for us and one for Grandmama. So we'd rush up to the gas station for the newspaper, but she didn't trust me enough to go inside and buy it because I might get one without the coupons and that's the only reason her and my grandmama wanted the newspaper in the first place. I remember one time I begged her to let me go inside and get the paper and like a dumb ass I got one without the coupons. She didn't speak to me for like two or three days.

So we leave the house, go back for the purse, get the

newspaper, and finally we get to church. We're walking to the door and my mom's doing that running-late marching thing again and going through her purse. We hit the steps and she looks over at me and she's been so busy rushin' all morning that she hasn't looked at me since breakfast, and much to her surprise, I looked a fuckin' mess. I got on some black slacks, dirty white tennis shoes, dried-up drool around my mouth, my nose is dirty, and, remember, I used water as grease to oil my hair up, so as a result my hair was nappy as hell! She'd get furious. "I thought I told you to comb your hair!" And I'd reply, "I did, got damn it!" Then she'd grab me by my arm. Remember when your mom would grab your arm and then hold it above your head and drag you to your destination? She'd do that. She'd drag me around to the side of the church and pull out a comb and then she'd go to town on me. For those of you who don't know, black hair gets nappy(er) after it gets wet, so my hair was super-duper nappy by now. So imagine this angry, runnin'-late woman who takes pride in "presentation" frantically combing my hair. There'd be sparks flying. Then she'd lick her hands and get all that crud out of my eyes, then unbutton my pants and tuck my shirt in waaay too deep with a blatant disregard for my testicles, button my pants back up and fasten my belt two notches too tight, and then she'd *brush me off* again and say, "Now take your little dirty behind in there and let's praise the Lord!"

MHD: Milton
Hand Day

March 13, 2004

To some, today is just another ordinary day, but to others
today is a very special time of year. Because today is
Bracket Sunday. For you non–basketball followers out
there, that means that today is the day they set the brack-
ets for the NCAA Tournament, the championship tournament for college basketball. Why is that a big deal? Well,
number one, it makes colleges, and television networks,
and shoe companies, and soft drinks, etc., etc., millions
and millions and millions of dollars. Number two, I like

to call it the Time of Facing the Challenge. It's the little guy trying to take down the big guy. It's the big guy trying to live up to expectations. It's a showcase for all the national superstars, and it's a time for unsung heroes to become household names. But most important, it was my father's favorite time of the year. It was a holiday to him. He didn't dig Christmas or Thanksgiving, never made a fuss over New Year's—well, except of course for the bowl games—but he loved tournament time. He watched every game he could. He'd even take off of work to watch the tournament. He made his bracket predictions, and he was pretty good too. He had a knack for picking the upsets. It was one of the few times of the year that he and I could really sit down together and hang out. So with this being the beginning of another tournament, could we please have a moment of silence in honor of my pops?

Thank You

One Word:

Christmas!

Now you know I couldn't write a book about growing up and whatnot without talking about the only thing that made a kid's life worth living. The only day in the year that matters. That's right, the granddaddy of them all, Christmas. Everybody loves Christmas. I mean, let's face it. Christmas is the shit. Now don't get me wrong. I know that's also the time of year where the suicide rate in America's at its highest because a lot of people are lonely and depressed losers, but fuck them. Everybody loves Christmas! Especially when you're a kid. For all the

bullshit us kids take all year round, Christmas makes it
damn near worth it. Christmastime is like *Girls Gone
Wild* for kids. Seriously. I can remember lying in my bed
late at night in the dark with a flashlight and a Sears catalog. The toy section of that Sears catalog was like porn
as far as I was concerned, and I'd sit there and fantasize
about the toys I wanted all night long. I was like a toy-
pimp. "Deez is my old toys, and deez right heeeerre, is
gon' be my new toys. And when my new toys get here
y'all old toys gonna have to gooooo. Cause I got me some
new toys, baby."

I approached Christmas with strategy like I was one
of those professional Las Vegas gamblers. I'ma ask Santa
for this. I'ma ask my mama for that. I had it covered.
Cause even though I believed in Santa Claus, my better
judgment told me that he needed a little help, cause
sometimes I'd see Santa Claus ringing the bell outside of
Wal-Mart begging for change and I'd be like, "Damn.
Reaganomics ain't shit. Santa Claus ain't got no business
workin' for the army." But just in case he did exist, I'd
make sure I buttered him up pretty good. I'd write him
notes like:

Hadjii
My House
Brunswick, Georgia 31520

                    Mr. Santa Claus
                    North Pole

January 1, 1981 [I always made sure I got an early jump on
Christmas]

Dear Santa Claus,

My mama told me that honesty is the best policy, so I'ma
be straight up wit'chou. I think you are the man! Now my
daddy says you ain't real and him and my mama the ones that
buy me all them presents, but I'm no fool. He's just sayin' that
cause you white and my daddy don't like givin' white people
no credit. I ain't like that. I'll give it to ya, Santa. You a bad
muthafucka for riskin' your life every year to give us black
kids presents. Ya know the brothas don't take too kindly to
folks breakin' into they houses. Especially fat white people.
Especially fat white people who let little kids sit in their lap
while they beg for "favors." A lot of us consider that type of
thing perverted. By the way, just how do you get up in our
house being that we ain't got no chimney? If you were black
you'd be in jail somewhere. I'm so tired of this double standard. Between racial inequality, an inadequate educational system, and Easter speeches it's enough to make a five-year-old
wanna holler. Gotta go.

Love,

Hadjii

P.S. I want some Transformers, some GI Joes, a BB gun, a
bike, a basketball, some Nikes, some He-Men, Castle
Greyskull, train set like the one Arnold's got on *Diff'rent
Strokes,* the conductor hat to go with it, some walkie-talkies,
a football, an Atari, some Atari games, a TV to play the Atari

on, some Spiderman stuff, some Batman stuff, some army men, some race cars, a racetrack, a remote-control car, a remote-control truck, a remote-control plane, a remote-control boat, some batteries to go with all that remote-control shit, some bunk beds so I can flip from the top bunk onto the bottom one, all the stuff off page 309 in the Sears catalog, the A-Team van, a puppy, a little brother, and a female manikin that I can keep under my bed that turns into a real woman when . . . well damn, Santa, some things should remain classified.

Now last year all I got was some underwear, a Big Wheel, and a Latin coloring book. Therefore, this year, to ensure satisfaction, I've taken the liberty of enclosing some photos of the items aforementioned as well as a couple of coupons. This year's theme: Keep that bullshit in the North Pole.

Tell Mrs. Claus I said hello,

Hadjii

Enclosure

Nah, I'm just playin'. I always had some good Christ-mases. Because what makes a good Christmas is if you got at least one gift from each of the three categories. Ya see, there are three categories of gifts. The first category is your main gift, which is the one you want the most. The big one. Ya know, like the bike or the video game or the BB gun. The main gift also usually costs the most, so you knew that if you didn't get it for Christmas you ain't have a chance in hell at gettin' it any other time of year.

The next bunch is called the throw-in gifts. These can be anything from cheap toys to clothes, a comic book here or there, some candy, posters, and stuff like that. And the throw-in bunch is very important because your mom's gotta hide the main gift from you all month to keep you in suspense; however, she's still gotta make it look like there's some shit under the tree. That's where the throw-in gifts come into play. You can make it look like a kid's got a thousand presents under the tree for twenty bucks.

And last but not—well actually it's least too—is the fi-nal category, which is called the must-haves and usually consists of a bunch of shit that you don't want or didn't even ask for, but it's just crap ya need, like underwear and undershirts. Trust me, my entire family knew I needed as many pairs of underwear in my life as possible.

And those are the three categories. Unless, of course, you had my dad for a father. He created his own special category of gifts that other kids didn't have to deal with, which was the "this is a present but it ain't really for your pleasure" gift. His presents always came with responsibilities or homework or some shit. Be somethin' I'd have to work at, like "Here's your drum set. Now learn how to play the drums!" "Here's ya keyboard. Your guitar. Your English-to-Spanish dictionary. Your Chinese-arithmetic game set." He'd give me shit like a golf club (one golf club) and then make me go out in the front yard and work on my stroke. Got me practicing on Christmas. He could take the fun outta anything.

So here's the scenario. Ya wake up on Christmas like around five-thirty in the morning and force ya parents to give you ya presents, right? Then you open ya presents until, oh, in my case, five-thirty-five, but you play with them until about one o'clock. Then it's showtime. Showtime's when all the kids in the neighborhood go outside and compare gifts. It's like your first Playa's Ball. So you go outside dribbling your basketball, or in my case, swinging my golf club. Now here comes Mario and Dave and they're the two kids in the neighborhood who got new bikes this year. That's always the shit. Can't go wrong wit' a new bike. Then ya got Damon, who's like the biggest kid in the neighborhood, so he always has to wait until Christmas to get some pants and shoes that actually fit. And he's so excited about his new wardrobe that he wears all of his new clothes over to your house so he can mess 'em up in the neighborhood Christmas football game whenever the kid who got the new football shows up. Then ya got the showoffs, Stacy/Tracy/Shannon/Jeremy/Jamie/Marion/Adrian/Chris. They don't come out Christmas Day, so you go over to their house only to discover that they're busy helping their daddy put together a trampoline, or a basketball goal, or the granddaddy of them all, a fuckin' go-cart. Damn I hate Stacy/Tracy/Shannon/Jeremy/Jamie/Marion/Adrian/Chris. They don't even know how good they've got it.

Last but not least, there's always the one dumb ass who comes walking up the street behind his new remote-control car. First of all, they can never drive'em straight, so they keep running the car all into your feet and shit. Messing up your mama's plants. Second of all, remote-control cars are bullshit, at least the ones we had. They couldn't do any of that shit you saw them doin' in the commercials. In the commercials remote-control cars be in rush-hour traffic with real cars and shit. Racing in the Daytona 500 in the rain. Driving through puddles and everything. Man, in the real world you drive your remote-control car through a puddle one time and you ain't got no remote-control car no more. And those remote-control airplanes were even worse. Every year somebody would get one and we'd be all excited to see that shit fly and all it would do was go real fast on the street for like two minutes trying to take off and then get like five inches off the ground and crash into your mama's car. Then somebody would say, "You're supposed to throw it in the air first. Then it'll fly." Okay. CRASH! No more plane. What a rip-off. Then ya had the gay kid who didn't know he was gay yet who'd come down the street wit' some gay shit like a Care-Bear kite. Little did he know his parents didn't get him a kite cause he wanted a kite. They got him a kite cause the gay kid who doesn't know he's gay yet is usually kind of chubby. So they figure he'll lose some weight runnin' around with that kite all the time. Parents think they're slick.

Girls never come out on Christmas morning. Know why? Because girls get a bunch of indoor shit for Christmas. Barbie dolls, toy ovens, pink mirrors, and dumb shit like that. They're too embarrassed to come outside. Guys are like, "Hey, check out my new bike!" Then girls say, "That's nothin'. Check out my new balloon. I blew it up myself." Girls get shitty Christmases. Then again, I guess I can't really talk, because after a girl would show me her shitty balloon I'd be like, "Check out this cool SAT study manual my dad got me."

And you learn a lot from Christmas, like, it really is better to give than to receive, because you know what the funniest thing about Christmas is? Giving your parents those bullshit presents that kids buy. Remember when you were in elementary school and a couple of days before Christmas instead of going to PE your class would go into this one room that had all these little dumbass items to buy as Christmas gifts for your parents? My mom would give me like seven dollars so I could get my Christmas shoppin' on, and you couldn't tell me shit! We'd go in that room and there'd be like five tables. One would have them little mini-Bibles and them statuettes of Jesus and Mary and the rest of the gang, and then there were the praying hands and whatnot. That's what I always bought for my grandparents. Anything with Jesus or Mahalia Jackson on it would do. Another table always had the little minitool sets and grooming kits with the little comb and toenail clippers. Then ya had the table that had the little plates that said some shit like "Merry Christmas," "Season's Greetings," or "Welcome to Las Vegas." And then for my favorite table, who can forget the one with them muthafuckin' snow globes? My mama got one of them Winter Wonderland snow globes from me every Christmas. I didn't give a damn. She seemed to enjoy that last snow globe so much. Now that I'm grown, that seems a little strange, because who in their right mind gives their mama or anybody for that matter a snow globe for Christmas? As a matter of fact, is there ever a good time to give somebody a snow globe? What the hell do you do with a snow globe? Shake it for thirty seconds and then watch the shit inside swirl around for a few minutes? That ain't exactly my idea of year-round fun. In all of my years on this earth I never saw my mama playin' wit' a fuckin' snow globe. We never had a conversation where my mom stopped and said, "Ya know what this house is missing? Ya know what my life is lacking? A snow globe." Needless to say, a minor detail like that ain't stop me! "Oh, she's gonna love this one. Look! This one's got Frosty the Snowman standing in the middle of New York City! That's classy!" And bless her heart, my mom was great, because she used to actually act like she appreciated getting that dumb shit from me. And I was such a sorry kid that I had the audacity to make my mom gift-wrap the snow globe the night before Christmas and then I'd put it under the tree like it was supposed to be a surprise. And do you know, she would still open that shit up on Christmas morning and act surprised? "Ahh. It's a snow globe! I love it." And then she'd hug me and then put the snow globe in like a special place. Ya know how every woman has those special places in the house like a mantel or something? Well we ain't have a mantel, but we had a china cabinet for yo ass. All of the special shit used to go in the china cabinet, and now not only did we have a china cabinet, but now we had a china cabinet with thirteen snow globes in that bitch.

And my daddy? Well, I don't know how it is for kids these days, but when I was growing up in the eighties, there was only one gift every father across the nation got for Christmas: Old Spice. Every year it was either some Old Spice or some Brut aftershave. I mean, damn, we were shopping at an elementary school, so it was either gonna be Old Spice or a minihammer. The Old Spice would win every time. The school couldn't keep that shit on the shelf. Every kid I knew bought their daddy Old Spice. Yet I've never bumped into a nigga on the street who smelled like Old Spice. It's like who shot JFK, what's the meaning of life, and who in the hell wears Old Spice? It's just one of those questions. I guess it's the same two or three niggas who still eat Spam. And my pops wasn't too big on formalities, so he had gotten to the point where he wouldn't even open his present anymore. One year he even said, "Look, I don't like Old Spice, and I don't shave. So next year, don't buy me anything. Now go to your room and play with that scientific calculator I gotcha."

And that would bother most people, but it was cool wit' me. Know why? Cause that meant I had more money for snow globes! Yeah, I'll give my mom this snow globe and this lovely ornament I made her that's really just a painted egg with my picture on it and a string attached to it. "Yeah, it's an ornament during Christmas, but once Easter rolls around all we have to do is cut the string off and then we can hide this mufucka! It's the gift that keeps on givin'. Now where's my bike?"

I always had to keep my parents focused on what was really important cause, well, they'd lose focus, meaning they'd forget what Christmas was all about. Me! However, there is one Christmas tradition that bugs me to this day, and I'm reminded of it every time I hear the words *Christmas tree.*

Now I don't really have any ill will toward the actual tree itself, but throughout my entire childhood, every year, like clockwork, the Battle of the Christmas Tree would take over our Home-Sweet-Home.

See, my mom and dad had a very good marriage because they had an understanding. My mom let my dad be the Man of the House and my pops recognized that she was the Queen of the Castle, which basically meant, "Hadjii, every now and then we're gonna have to let'er hang some pink shit up." They compromised, they shared, and they did their best to be in agreement on almost everything, but year after year all hell would break loose whenever it was time for the Christmas tree battle.

It always started like this. It would be like a Thursday or Friday night and my mom would tell me we were going to get a Christmas tree the next day. Then my dad would chime in and say, "I don't know why we've gotta buy a Christmas tree every year. Doesn't make any sense. Every year we spend thirty, forty, fifty bucks on a tree only to have it up for a week or two and then throw it out. What we need to do is just spend some money on an artificial tree that we can use over and over again." And my mom would be like, "I don't like artificial trees. They don't even smell. Besides, who wants to pull a tree out of a box?" So my mom and I would go out on our usual Saturday grocery shopping and that evening we'd go to like a Christmas tree farm and pick out a nice tree and bring it home. End of story, right? Wrong.

My mom would want to decorate the tree her way and my dad wanted to decorate the tree his way. My mom wanted to use white lights. My dad thought white lights were boring, "The tree needs some color." My dad wanted blinking lights. My mom thought blinking lights were tacky, and besides, "If you've got two lines of blinking lights on a tree they won't blink in unison." He wanted a tall and skinny tree. She wanted a short and bushy tree. She wanted to leave the lights on all night. He wanted to turn 'em off when we went to bed. And on and on and on. So much so to the point where they'd actually argue over this shit like brother and sister and I'd always get stuck in the middle. Used as leverage if you will. My mom would be like, "Well, I want a Christmas tree and Hadjii does too. Dontcha, Hadjii?" And I'd be like, "Hell yeah, cause if we ain't got no tree where the fuck am I gonna put this snow globe?" And you know when you're a kid you don't wanna see your parents fighting, so I'm like five years old and I find myself getting emotional. I'd start crying and shit and of course my mom being the cunning woman she is would try to use this to her advantage.

> MOM: (to my father) Well, I hope you're happy. I
> really hope you're happy. You've made Hadjii cry.
> Why are you crying, Hadjii?
> ME: Cause I want'chall to stop fighting.
> MOM: Ya hear that? The boy wants white nonblinkin'
> lights on a short, stubby Christmas tree!

But my dad, being the cunning man he was, had a response.

> DAD: Yeah, but by the time he turns eighteen, we
> ain't gonna be able to send him to college, cause yo
> ass done spent thirteen million dollars on
> Christmas trees over the years.

That didn't convince me, but he'd always win me over with this next point.

> DAD: Besides, all the money you're spendin' on trees
> could've been used to buy the boy more presents.

ME: (wiping tears away) . . . More presents?

DAD: Yeah, your mom wasted fifty dollars over this
tree that we coulda been spendin' on you.

ME: Well, I'll be damned. Mama, that's some selfish
shit.

MOM: What?

ME: Don't what me. I'm just glad the truth is finally
comin' out. You're up here spendin' money on
temporary shit that comes and goes, while we
could've been putting that money toward
something with some longevity, like those sea
monkeys I've been wanting.

MOM: Okay, fine then. I can't have my tree the way I
want it? Well, I think there's some tuna and Pop
Tarts in the cupboard. Y'all two noncookin'
monkeys have fun.

Then she'd storm out of the room and I'd turn to my
daddy and say, "Ya know? If we don't ever learn how to
cook she's just gonna keep pullin' this shit. One day
we're gonna look up and this whole fuckin' house is
gonna be pink."

Eventually it got to the point where I even became the
adult in the situation. I'd be in my room and hear them
arguing and come out and say, "What's goin' on here?!"
And they'd say, "Nothin'." Then I'd say, "Well it don't
sound like nothin'. Sounds to me like y'all arguin' over
that damn tree again. Now since y'all two don't seem to
be mature enough to handle the responsibility of havin' a
Christmas tree, I guess we just ain't gonna have one this

year. Ah-ah-ah. Stop that whining. This hurts me more than it hurts you. Call the neighbors over and see if they're in need of a tree. Give it to some folks who know how to appreciate things."

Y'all think I'm playin', but this used to be a serious issue in our house year after year. I can remember years where we ain't even get a real tree and my mom had to put the presents under an eggplant. That wasn't a good year. Then there was the year we had two trees. His and hers. But the worst was Christmas of '84. That year will forever go down in infamy, cause that's the year the shit really went down.

I was probably seven or eight years old and I'm still in elementary school, so my dad was still picking me up after school. At least on the days he remembered to. So one day we get home and for some reason, I mean like I said before, my mom would always buy the tree on Thursday or Friday or Saturday, so she could decorate it over the weekend, but I guess she got too busy this particular year. Maybe a friend died and she had to cook chicken or somethin', but usually when she bought a tree, we'd bring it home and put it in the backyard overnight and then bring it in and decorate it the next day.

But for some reason, she bought a tree and, like I said, she must've been busy or somethin' because the tree sat in the backyard for like two or three days. So my daddy, being the brilliant man he was, came up with this bright idea. He brings me home from school one day, and after eating a bowl or two of leftover chicken, pecan, tomato, pork chops, onions, and pinto bean soup (that was my pop's idea of cooking, just take all of the old shit in the refrigerator that's about to be thrown out, put it in a big pot, add water, and now you've got *Daddy's Soup*), I'm feeling slightly buzzed. Then he suggests that we should decorate the tree ourselves and give your mama a break this year. It'll be a surprise. Little did I know he was seizing this opportunity to fulfill all his dirty little tree fantasies. This nigga took my mom's tree and hung every blinking light within a block on it. We had traffic lights on that bitch. Turn signals, camera flashbulbs, flashlights, lightning bugs, police sirens. If it blinked or flashed, it was on the tree. And when we were done my dad turned to me and asked me if I liked it, and I wasn't quite sure yet. Then he said, "See, it has character now." And instantly I said, "Oh shit."

Now even though I was only a youngster I was pretty good at word association. So I knew that whenever my father used the word *character,* something was fucked up. For example, I played basketball one year at the Boys' Club. We were the Boys' Club Jazz. All the other teams were named something cool like the Boys' Club Lakers, Hoyas, Blue Devils, Tigers, or Cobras or some shit, and lo and behold our team was named the muthafuckin' Boys' Club Jazz. And we were sorry as hell! We went one and eleven. For you non–sport fans out there that means we lost eleven games and only won one, and I swear to you, the only reason we won that one was because the team we were supposed to be playin' that day didn't show up! I promise. They were this team of white boys from some Christian school who didn't believe in wearing shorts, so they used to come and kick our ass in their jeans and khakis and shit, and they were a guaranteed win for everyone except us. We were the only team they ever beat, and they probably would've beaten us again, except they didn't show up. And ya know what my father said after that miserable season? "Hadjii, I know it's been a tough season, but look on the bright side. Everybody's gotta lose sometimes. It builds character." That was his excuse for everything. I'd be like, "Mama, these jeans you bought me only have one leg. I can't wear this shit to school." And he'd say, "Oh Hadjii, I know the kids are gonna fuck with ya and you'll probably getcha ass kicked a couple of times, but hey, it builds character." So when he said our Christmas tree had character I knew it was gonna be downhill from there.

My mom came home that evening, and I've never thought of my pops as a stupid man, but he did have a major flaw. He didn't always realize what was going on at the moment. I can say this because when my mom walked in and saw this ugly-ass tree, this dude had the nerve to say, "Tah-dahhh!" Like she was supposed to be impressed. I was a kid and even I knew you don't say "tah-dah" to somebody unless you know they're gonna like it. I never came home with a bunch of F's on my report card and said some damn "tah-dah!" My mom stood there in the doorway in complete silence. Then she looked at this ugly-ass tree covered in blinking lights and duct tape, then she looked at him, then what really messed me up was that she looked at the tree again, and then she looked at me and said, "Hadjii, did you have anything to do with this?" And now I'm in a real bind because I look over at my daddy and he's grabbing his belt buckle like, "Yeah Hadjii, did you have anything to do with this?" Now I'm thinkin', Okay, presents or ass-whuppin? I can side with my dad and avoid the ass-whuppin or go with Mom and get some presents. Decisions, decisions. Alright, Daddy, come on and make it quick.

I duN Wint aNd Got Me wun Of Dem Edumakashuns

I don't mean to be arrogant or nothin', so I hope I don't offend anybody with this next statement, but graduating from high school really wasn't that big of a deal to me. Don't get me wrong. I definitely understand that it's harder for some people than it is for others, and I was fortunate enough to be one of those others. School came naturally for me. I never really had to apply myself. That's probably the biggest beef me and my parents ever had, because they knew I could've done better, but in all honesty, I did just enough to get by.

I ended up graduating with something like a B average anyway. And even though it wasn't a big deal to me, it was a big deal to my family. Not in the sense that I had made it, but in the sense that this was like my first step toward making it.

So I went to my graduation, and afterward ya know there's always the kid who's throwing the bomb-ass graduation party, which was gonna be followed the next day by the bomb-ass graduation pool party, which was gonna be followed by the bomb-ass graduation crab-boil after the pool party. And my uncle, who still had the spirit of a ladies' man in 'em, had just bought a brand-new Mercedes-Benz, and this cat, knowing how big a weekend this was going to be, had the courage to say, "Hadjii, for your graduation I'm gonna let'chou pimp my new ride for the weekend."

"WHAT?!" I replied.

"Yeah, keep it for the weekend and give it back to me on Sunday." And of course, "If you wreck it, I'ma tap that ass!"

"Cool," I replied.

After the graduation ceremony, I was slippin' and slidin' through the city streets of Brunswick, Georgia, in a mean-ass Benz. Y'all know how to do it. Right hand grippin' the wheel, left hand on chin, windows down, music pumpin', and takin' corners slow. I'm drivin' a Benz, got dammit. My car was an '86 Dodge Colt that used to idle when you tried to turn it off. For those of you out there who've never had a piece of shit car in your life, when I say my car used to idle, I mean that when you parked my car and turned it off, it would go into like this five-minute seizure or some shit and make noises like boom-boom-boom while it was shaking and coughing. Remember that booty dance Beyoncé used to do? Well, imagine my car doin' that. Isn't quite as sexy. It's gotta be in the top ten of the most embarrassing conditions you can have. Right up there with impotence, halitosis, and having ugly kids, so to give the Colt up for the weekend in exchange for a Benz was quite a moment in my life.

Because you know how it is when you go from driving your raggedy-ass car to a car that actually works. First of all you never wanna drive your car again. Second, you find yourself driving a lot faster than you usually would. Especially when you're seventeen years old.

And I'm proud as hell, cause number one, I'm in a Benz, and number two, I've got my diploma laying pretty on the passenger seat. Benz and a diploma. Can't nobody tell me shit right now! I'm leanin' and lookin' cool with my diploma ridin' shotgun, and then, much to my dismay, the next thing I know, I hear a police siren behind me. So after I drive a couple more feet (like ten miles) to make sure I'm his target, I pull over. Then the officer gets out of his car and walks up to my window and asks for my license and registration. I pull my license out of my wallet and lean over to get the registration out of the glove compartment. That's when the officer notices my diploma on the passenger seat.

So I give'em my license and I give'em the registration.

The officer takes it. Big ole surly white dude, and I can say he was surly because ya know I tried to talk myself out of the shit first, but he wasn't hearin' it, and anybody who can resist my charm is surly. So I give everything to 'em, and he looks at my license, and then he looks in the car. He looks at my license, and then he looks in the car. He looks at my license, and then he looks in the car. Then for one more time, he looks at my license, and then he looks at me and says, "Son, lemme tell ya somethin'. I've been a police officer for thirty-seven years. On highway patrol for thirty-four years. I've seen anything and everything. So you've gotta wake up pretty early in the mornin' to sneak one past me. So tell the truth. You stole that diploma, didn't ya?"

Gotcha!

Is It Just Me or Do We Need a Longer Shortbus?

When I hear a parent tell their kid that high school's gonna be some of the best years of their life, I cringe. As soon as they walk away, I grab that kid and tell'em, "No disrespect intended, but your mom ain't necessarily the sharpest knife in the drawer." Actually, if your mom or dad says some stupid shit like that they must be one sandwich short of a picnic in my opinion, because high school has absolutely, positively, got to be one of the most confusing and chaotic stages that you could ever expect a young person to perform on. Everybody's bodies are changing. Personalities are changing. The rules and laws are changing. Requirements and standards are changing. The world is changing. You think you know a lot, but you're really dumb as hell, but you're not as dumb as everybody thinks you are. Then on the other hand, if you're fortunate enough to be a part of that *Talented Tenth* you've got all these adults promising you things like guaranteed success. I mean after all, if you can make an A in science then surely you can become a biochemist. Right? Right? Yeah, right. All your teachers flatter you with their compliments, but they're not really helpin' you make anything happen. They're just passing you on to the next stage. See, I'm talking about high school, but the shit goes south way before then, cause I got news for ya. The difference between your child becoming a lawyer someday or your child needing a lawyer someday takes place around second or third grade. Basically, your kid has three years to get their shit together. If they're white, they might get four. This is how it works:

Your kid shows up for kindergarten. As long as he or she can do the whole ABC thing, learn the Pledge of Allegiance, and stop pissin' on themselves, they'll be fine. Then ya get to first grade. In first grade you're picking up on some new concepts. Reading, writing, and the math's getting a little more intense. That's where we start separating the men from the boys so to speak. Then ya got second grade. Here's the trick. By the time your kid hits third grade, if he or she isn't performing at a certain level, regardless of the reason, if you're not aware of what's goin' on as a parent, they're gonna put ya kid in the class with no windows. Now I ain't cryin' racism, but I honestly do think white kids get more of a fair shot. If a white kid acts crazy in class and he's hyper, they'll say, "He has an enthusiasm for life." And teachers would say that old-woman-teacher shit like, "Boy, I wish I could bottle up some of that energy for myself. Ha-ha-ha." But when a black kid acts crazy in class, we slap a helmet on his head. White kids paint on the wall and they're artistic or unique, black kids paint on the wall and they're troublemakers with a disregard for public property.

Anyway, once your kid hits third grade, teachers and the powers that be decide where they think your child is best suited. So they put all of the smart kids on one track, all the normal kids on another track, and then they take all the crazy kids and stick them over on that crazy hall. The crazy kids have got their own wing in school, so by the time they get to high school, all the smart kids are excited about life and their possibilities, all the normal kids are just ready to get it over with, most of the other kids have gone crazy, and all the crazy kids are about three days away from posing for their first mug shots.

See, the thing about teachers is they want everybody to be lions and tigers. In our world, that means doctors and lawyers. But what about all the people out there who are bears, gators, and eagles? Like architects, account-

ants, and interior decorators? What about nurses, teachers, and chefs? What about bus drivers, trashmen, and
store clerks? We need all of these people to make life
what it is. But if you listen to your schoolteachers as a
kid, they'll have you convinced that if you're not on track
to be a doctor or a lawyer you ain't gonna amount to anything. And who wants to hear that every day? That's why
people don't go to church, because even though they may
believe in God, they don't wanna hear anybody tell them
how fucked up they are every Sunday. So if a kid's already struggling in school and teachers are basically
telling him that he's a loser on a daily basis, a kid's like,
"Fuck it. I know when I'm not wanted." You'd probably
drop out too.

Truth is, there are only four days of school that even
count to a kid: (1) the first day of school, (2) the last day
of school, (3) school picture day, and (4) the day the
yearbook comes out.

That's it. Report card days and all those other necessary evils don't mean anything to a kid, but you better
believe we've got school picture day circled on our calen-
dars, buddy. We took picture day very seriously. You
never ran home with your report card. You never made a
big deal out of it when you made a good grade on your
test, unless of course you were dumb and couldn't believe you actually passed PE. But shiiit, when you got the
information on your picture packets you'd check out of
school early.

But as much as I may have hated school, I still didn't

mind going, cause that's where all my friends were. You remember those days where you stayed home from school? I used to wake up, like every other day, not wanting to go, then after begging and concocting some fake vomit, I would finally get to stay home. I would sleep until about eleven o'clock only to wake up and realize that there wasn't shit for me to do because everybody I knew was at school. That is of course unless I felt like robbin' a gas station with all my thug drop-out friends, but being that I was never really into any of that, I guess I came as close to liking school as a normal kid could.

Especially once I got to like sixth grade, cause that's when you got your first taste of what they called related-arts classes. See, related-arts classes were classes like Home Economics, where you first learned how to make pigs in a blanket and boil water. Then ya had Woodshop, where sixth graders got a chance to work with sharp items without getting arrested. You had music, which is always a crowd pleaser, and there was also the Business class that taught you how to type, how to write a check, balance a checkbook, and what have you. They never taught you how to make money, but they were experts on spendin' it.

Then adults go on to make the junk even worse because whenever you and your family get together, they ask ya somethin' that you don't know the answer to, then they say, "Damn, boy. What they teachin' you at that school? You don't know shit. Boy, when I was yo age I knew how to tailor my own clothes and everything."

That's when I usually ask, "Well if your education was so much better than mine, then how come you can't set the clock on the microwave, ya fuckin' brainiac?"

The other thing that used to piss me off was when I'd come home from school every now and then all amped up because I thought I learned some new shit that I could apply to my life and those around me only to find that even though it may be true, it didn't always apply. Like one day this lady came to our class and spoke about the dangers of tobacco. And she said, "If your mommy or daddy smokes, you should hide their cigarettes. That way they'll know how much you love them. Then once they see that, they'll quit to show their love for you." So like a dumb ass I went home and hid my dad's smokes from him, and needless to say, love hurts, and my daddy was very good at showing how much he *loved* me.

Shortly after that this lady came to our class and taught us about domestic violence. Shit, I couldn't wait to get home. I had a newfound confidence. I went in the living room and said, "Uhh, look here, Daddy. Today in school this lady came to our class and dropped some science on a nigga." He said, "Oh yeah? Tell me all about it."

"Well, ya know how every time before I get a whuppin you say it's because you love me? Well, she said that, uhh, if a man lays his hands on a woman or a child, that's not love."

He said, "Oh yeah?"

"Yep."

"What else you learn today?"

"Well, funny that you'd ask because I also learned that it's illegal to spank children in the state of Georgia." (Now I didn't know if this was true, but I saw a window of opportunity.) "That's right. It's a new day, nigga. If you ever touch me again I will have Georgia's finest down here to deal wit'cho ass, buddy. How do ya like them apples?"

And he said, "Wow, I didn't know that. I guess I'm gonna have to change my ways."

"You got damn right." And to make a long story short, that nigga drove me to Florida and beat the shit outta me.

But school still had its perks, because I grew up in the eighties, and in the eighties the news was "the news." Like now, the news feels the need to embellish and tries to make stories out of stuff like bird flu, and I ain't never seen no sneezin' bird or nothin'. Mad cow? I didn't even know cows had feelings. But when I was a kid the news didn't have to embellish shit. The facts were enough to scare the daylights out of you. And I don't mean that little bullshit local news about high school football and local government. I'm talkin' about that seven–seven-thirty news. Talkin' about when Dan Rather and Tom Brokaw and them niggas came on TV and scared the shit out of you. Because if Dan Rather said it, that was yo ass! You'd turn to Channel 4 and just see Dan Rather looking down at his notes. Then he'd shake his head for a minute and then look up and say, "It's called Acquired Immune Deficiency Syndrome . . . AIDS, and it's sweeping the nation." And then you walked outside and your whole neighborhood was HIV positive. Then Tom Brokaw said they got this new shit out called crack, word on the street is everybody's doin' it. And then you walked outside and everybody was smoking crack. It was crazy. But it made school more interesting because every now and then something would be going on in the world and then all the schools would be forced to work that shit into the curriculum.

Like, remember when Nancy Reagan came up with that "Just Say No to Drugs" campaign and all the sudden we all had to write poems and jingles about why kids shouldn't do drugs and shit? Remember that? Remember that public service announcement that had the dude trying to sell drugs to the first graders and shit and it had everybody thinking that all the drug dealers were hanging out at the schools trying to sell their six-year-olds crack? News flash. That's false. Know why? Sure, maybe there are some drug dealers out there who would be ruthless enough to sell crack to first graders, if it weren't for one problem. First graders ain't got no fuckin' money. And why the hell would somebody wanna sell some crack to some loudmouth-ass kid anyway? Can you imagine what Show 'n' Tell would've been like?

Anyway, we were in third grade in 1983 or somethin' like that, and none of us were even thinkin' about doin' any drugs until one day when we thought our teacher was walking us to our PE class, then the next thing ya know we're sitting on the floor in the middle of the library in front of some police officer who had a suitcase full of all types of cool shit. Crack, weed, needles, hash, heroin, cocaine, mushrooms, acid, PCP, angel dust, aerosol cans, gas tanks, Magic Markers, balloons, glue, spray paint, and WD-40. This nigga opened up a whole new world to us! But I digress.

Anyway, for some reason Nancy Reagan thought us third graders were their number one clientele, so we had to write antidrug poems that'll put a stop to this epidemic, like

Drugs are bad.
They're not good.
Just say "No!"

And then ya had

You won't get hugs
If you do drugs.
Don't be a fool.
Stay in school.
When you laugh
And when you cheer
You do not need
Liquor or beer.
Just say "No!"

Of course, I raised the ante with a haiku.

Drugs are not our friends,
They kill people and are mean.
Hot dogs taste better . . .

Then there were other times when school was off the chain for real. Like once a year they'd fuck around and lose their minds and let us do a week of pottery. Pottery was the shit. The art teacher would come out with a pot she'd made, and then she'd have like a couple of bowls, a vase, and all this other cool stuff she'd made out of clay. And ya know what's cool about artsy people who make stuff outta clay? Whenever they show you what they made, they always end the sentence by whispering *out of clay*. Like this is an Egyptian bowl I made *out of clay*. Check out this computer I made *out of clay*. And we'd all be like, "Hell yeah!" So when she said, "This week I'm gonna show you guys how to make some neat stuff that you can give to your parents," I was like, "That's what's up. I'm gonna make my mama a radio. And I'ma put some of them Aztec folk on the side of that shit. It's on and poppin'! Fuck them snow globes. Where's my clay?" Then the teacher said, "Oh, I'm sorry, Hadjii. I just thought we'd start off with something simple for our first time. You can make either a mug or a bowl." "A mug or a bowl?" Let me see, my mama doesn't drink any coffee, and she doesn't really eat soup either, but uhh, I guess she does knock down a couple shots of hot chocolate from time to time. Let's go mug. I mean, I can still fit one or two of them Aztec niggas on the side of a mug, can't I?

Ya ever seen somebody making pottery on television or in a movie and they've got the pottery or clay or whatever ya call it spinning, and they're molding it into its shape with their hands all smooth, and it looks all pretty and seductive and graceful? Think about Demi Moore in *Ghost*. Well, it doesn't quite go down like that when you're a kid. In all honesty there wasn't a damn thing graceful or smooth about my mug. The teacher tried to be encouraging, but I wasn't buyin' it. I'm like, "Why's it leaning to the side like that?" and she was like, "Don't worry about it. It's gonna be fine after we put it in the oven. That's when it takes its shape. Then we'll glaze it. Just wait until you see this mug tomorrow. You're gonna love it."

Boy, I'll tell ya, adults can be some lyin' muthafuckas when pottery's involved. My mug ain't come out lookin' like none of the mugs in my mama's cabinet, but you better believe I wasn't gonna let a little thing like hideousness stop me from givin' it to her. Cause ya know how if you look at anything long enough, eventually, it'll start looking okay? My mug was a piece of shit when I first saw it that morning, but by lunch it was looking pretty high-quality, buddy. By three o'clock I was thinking, "I wonder how much I can get for this bitch on the black market?" Cause the longer you look at it, the more you begin to rationalize and reason with ya failure. Like how people burn the chicken and call it Cajun. I was lookin' at my mug thinking, "Ya know, ain't every mug gotta have a handle on it. And ya know what? Just cause it's got that hole in the bottom doesn't mean ya can't drink out the muthafucka. Who made that shit up? Just gotta use a coaster. And tell me this stick man doesn't look just like an Aztec. This mug has character.

That night I found out just how much my mama loved me. I went in the kitchen like,

ME: Mama! Got something for ya!
MOM: Another snow globe?
ME: Snow globe? What? You think it's Christmas or
   somethin'? This is one of them "just because"
   presents. Now close ya eyes. They closed? Don't
   open'em. They still closed?

Ya know it takes ya like five minutes to pull that heavy-ass mug out'cha bookbag.

ME: Alright. Open'em!

My mom would open her eyes and then once again give another Oscar-worthy performance.

MOM: Ahh! For me? It's beautiful. I've been
needin' one of these!
ME: For real?
MOM: Yes. I've always wanted this . . . this . . . this
   thing. For when I do what I do where I need to
   have one of these, and now I've got one. Thank you.

Then she gave me a hug thinking it was over, but I was like, *We're just getting started, baby.*

ME: Okay, now drink somethin' out of it.
MOM: What?

ME: Drink out of it.

MOM: Hadjii, you don't drink out of something as
    nice as this.

ME: Why not? It's a mug.

MOM: It's a mug?

ME: Yeah. What'chou think it was?

MOM: (guilty) Oh? Uhh? I thought it was a cup.

ME: Yeah, cause it ain't got no handle, huh?

MOM: Yeah. But ya know, I'm really not that thirsty
    right now, and this mug is sooo big and heavy and
    ya know what? I know it's ten o'clock at night, but
    you know how you're always asking us to give you
    more freedom?

ME: Yeah.

MOM: Well, why don't you go down the street
    and play with those nice men on the corner for a
    while?

ME: Okay. I'll go right after I see you drink out of it.
    Hurry up!

Finally she gave in. She held her hand under the
bottom to keep the water in. Then she put it up to her
mouth and tried to drink out of it. Water was dribbling
all down her shirt, and I'm thinking, "That ain't supposed to happen, is it? My mama done broke my got
damn mug."

MOM: Umm-mm. That was gooood.

ME: Glad ya liked it. Well, I gotta go get my dice and
    then I'm headed to the corner.

I was on cloud nine. At least that's until my daddy found a way to add his own charm and signature to the situation. Later that night, after I had taken my bath and had come back out to tell my folks goodnight, I guess my mom was in the bedroom and hadn't filled my pops in on the whole mug concept yet. I walked into the living room and lo and behold I see my father, sitting in his chair using my dear and precious mug for an ashtray!

And usually I was a pretty calm, cool, and collected nine-year-old, but at the sight of this monstrosity, I must admit, I became slightly livid.

ME: Uhh, excuse me, Daddy, but have you lost yo
    fuckin' mind? Does that look like a muthafuckin'
    ashtray to you? Well, I guess so, cause you dumpin'
    ya ashes in it, but damn! Show some respect for
    other people's property! How's Mama gonna drink
    out of it now? You done— (pause) Wait a minute?
    Y'all in cahoots on this shit, aintcha?

A Short Story
About a Long
Twenty-four Hours

It really wasn't until I got to be about eleven or twelve that my mom and I really developed our relationship. For the most part when I was little, it was all about my daddy. He taught me how to tie my shoes and swing a bat. We played video games together. He took me fishing, and put up a basketball goal for me. We used to watch those Godzilla vs. Mothra and kung fu movies together as well as just television in general. He used to tell me what was good television, like *Hill Street Blues* and *Taxi*. And he used to hate a lot of the shows that I liked, like *Good Times* and *Three's Company*, cause he thought they were fake. He hated the idea of black people who were content with living in the projects and really hated that Jack Tripper on *Three's Company* had never banged any of his roommates. Janet, Crissy, Cindy, Terri, he should've gotten at least one of 'em. Come on, Jack. Damn!

Anyway, when I turned fifteen, a lot of my friends were turning sixteen and seventeen, so they had their driver's licenses. Some of 'em were even getting cars. This included my cousin, who'll remain nameless. He had a Buick with the bass in the back. You couldn't tell us shit. And we'd be slippin' and slidin' down the mean city streets on the weekend, us and a few of the fellas, and we started getting that urge to drink. Ya know how it is once ya get to a certain age, you think you're supposed to be drinking and shit? And there was this one corner store that would sell anybody, and I mean anybody, beer. You ain't need no ID or nothin'. You didn't even need a mustache. The only catch was, they knew you were underage, so they'd charge you like twenty dollars for a six-pack. What were you gonna do?

So one night we were goin' out, and you know I had to get fresh, right? Now when I say "get fresh," I mean just that. Get fresh. I don't know how it is for you white cats out there, but black people take getting dressed very seriously. Everybody thinks women are the only ones preoccupied with their looks. That's a lie. Cause you haven't seen anybody gettin' dressed until you've seen a young black dude get dressed. We be in the mirror talkin' shit to imaginary niggas who ain't even there. "Oh! They ain't ready for me tonight! I'm finna bust they ass tonight! They thought it was a game, but I ain't playin'! Look at this sweater! See how the red brings out the sexy in my lips? These girls finna go nuts! I'm liable to not have any more friends after tonight, cause I'm so fly I make niggas uncomfortable. Wait a minute. Oh, don't do it to 'em, Hadjii. I said don't do it to 'em, Hadjii! You tryin' to start a riot or somethin'? I thought you promised everybody you were gonna take it easy on 'em. You said you were gonna tone it down to give these other dudes hope, and look at you now. The suicide rate's about to go up all because of you. Hold up. I know you ain't finna put that watch on. Don't hit'em with the watch! The world ain't ready for the watch. Aww shit! This nigga done broke out the watch! When's it gonna end? Oh no. Not the belt. You gonna hit'em with the belt? Hadjii, they're gonna hate you if you put the belt on. He done went and put the belt on! Hadjii, are you gonna give these niggas any room to breathe? I mean how-how many women are you tryin' to take tonight? Stop the madness! Ladies and gentlemen, I haven't seen freshness like this since . . . since . . . Since? I've never seen anyone this fresh in the history of man! This dude is a fashion juggernaut." And just where are we taking all of this freshness tonight? To my high school's basketball game, of course.

So I put all my fresh-to-death necklaces on (I admit it, I used to wear like five or six gold necklaces at a time—I know it was lame, but it was the style back then), and I put my fresh-to-death shirt on (I had this one brown shirt that used to guarantee me at least four compliments and two phone numbers), I put my fresh-to-death jeans on (some dark-dark-ass navy blue Bugle Boy jeans that got me another phone number), and us and some friends (cause it took like fifteen of us to come up with twenty dollars) are hanging. We bought some beer, cause we wanna have a little buzz before we go to our game, and then went to Burger King to get something on our stomachs. Being that I had already spent my college tuition on buying the beers in the first place, I didn't have any money for food, but I was alright, or so I thought.

After the game, we hooked up with some of the older cats. Seniors. We were moving up in the world. They invited us to come over to this dude's house where they were gonna do some real drinking after the game. This was it. The Big Time. So we go over there and of course they're drinking, but they weren't drinking beer. They were drinking mixed drinks. "What'chall drinkin'?" I asked. "Golden Grain," the host replied. "Want some?" "Hell yeah! Fix me up." And I drank and drank, and sat and sat, and drank and drank some more. Mind you, I was fifteen, and I hadn't had anything to eat, and Golden Grain is like a 150 proof and I weighed like 155 pounds. See where I'm going with this?

After drinking we got back in the car and drove off.

My cousin turns the music up and we're chillin', but who would've thought that combining an empty stomach, 150 proof liquor, and bass could be so harmful to a nigga's digestive system? I threw up all over my boy's backseat. I'm throwin' up everything I had eaten since I'd been alive! I'm throwin' up baby food from fourteen years ago, I'm throwin' up fuckin' air. Ya know them dry heaves that feel like ya small intestine's tryin' to jump outta ya mouth? I'm throwin' up everything. Good thing I wasn't pregnant or that woulda probably popped out too.

And my cousin who hadn't even been drinking still managed to come up with the dumbest idea of the evening, because he believed that I'd feel better if I got something on my stomach. "Let's take'em to McDonald's," he says. Yeah, let's add grease to this equation, nigga. We pull up in the parking lot and he tells me to stay in the car. Okay, he orders me, "Stay in the fuckin' car!" "Okay," I replied, but then when they went inside, I felt lonely sittin' in the car all by myself, plus, I don't want no pickles on my burger. I think they need to know that. So I get my drunk ass out the car, and ya know how McDonald's usually has the curb or the elevated sidewalk or whatever you wanna call it? Well, you gotta step up to get on that sidewalk or whatever, and I swear I did, but I mistimed it and tripped over the curb. You ever been so drunk that as you're falling face first toward some concrete, not only do you forget to use your hands to break your fall, but you don't even remember to close your eyes? My eyes were open on the way down with my face like two inches away from the concrete and I was thinking, "This is gonna hurt." But actually, I didn't feel a fuckin' thing. I heard it, but I didn't feel it. And then there's a security guard outside watching all of this take place and I guess he's too busy laughing at me to take any real action.

But now we had another problem. I couldn't go home lookin' like that. Sand particles all on my face and shit. My parents just might get suspicious. Because even though there are a lot of parents out there who smoke weed and get drunk with their kids, my parents weren't one of 'em. Which I'm glad about, because who in the hell wants to get drunk with their parents? I mean, when I'm drinkin' I wanna sit around and crack jokes, talk about women, reminisce, and all that kind of stuff. How am I supposed to do that with my daddy? "Boy, lemme tell ya how I had ya mama last night!" I don't wanna hear that shit.

So my brainiac of a cousin thinks he's on a roll by now and comes up with yet another bright idea. "Hey, let's take'em back to thang's house and clean'em up." So we go back to the dude's house we were just drinking at. Criminals always return to the scene of the crime. Once we were there they took me to the bathroom. They wash my face and all that, and then I think they walked out to use the phone or something, and ya know those old-fashioned sinks that just hang out from the wall with no cabinet under 'em or anything? Well, that's what they had. And I swear that what happened next would've happened no matter who had leaned on the sink. It just so happened that I was the next contestant on this fucked-up game show, because I leaned on the sink and bam! The shit fell out of the wall! I don't think you heard me. I said, the sink FELL OUT OF THE WALL! Water was squirting everywhere! And I was so drunk I just stood there. So now dude had to give me a pair of his jeans to wear, which was very cool of him. Only problem was, I'm like five foot nine at the time and he's six-six. So now I'm drunk, smelling like liquor and vomit, walking around in jeans five sizes too big, and like an hour past curfew.

On top of that, it's Friday night and my parents don't go to sleep until I get home. Not that they didn't trust me or were worried about me. Everybody knows Hadjii would never do anything stupid, right? Whatever. My parents knew they had a nut on their hands, so I had to check in when I got home. I mean, just in case I were to do something out of character like come home drunk out of my skull, for example.

We pulled up in our driveway. Wait, I mean we pulled up in our yard, and my cousin escorted me to the door and tried to prop me up against the rail like he wanted to play the doorbell game. Ya remember the one where ya used to go up to somebody's house, ring the doorbell, and take off runnin'? Yeah, that one. But it's a little harder to pull off when ya got a big-ass Buick behind ya, so he had to play it cool. Now we've always had a weird lock on our front door that's tricky as hell to open. To this day, even sober, I have a hard time unlocking our front door, so imagine how difficult it was for my cousin who's trying to open the door with one hand while holding me up with the other while being scared as shit. So as I was trying to show him what key to use, and how ya gotta jiggle it, and say, "Open, sesame," and all this shit, my mom heard us fumbling with the doorknob, so she opened the door for us and greeted us with the proclamation, "Y'all been drinkin'." And I'm thinkin', "Damn, is this chick some kinda bloodhound or somethin'? I done ate seventeen muthafuckin' peppermints. She need to get a job sniffin' luggage or some shit."

Now my cousin, who's far from being a dumb cat, is still trying to walk me to my room and, like I said, he's not a dumb cat, but he was about to ask one of the dumbest questions I've ever heard in my life. He turns to my mom and says, "Hey Auntie. How ya doin'?" My mom replies, "What's wrong with my son?" (Note: When parents disregard your name and call you by a word like boy, girl, nigga, etc., you know things aren't good. For example: "My son's in jail!," "My daughter's pregnant?," "My baby's a Republican?" Things are about to get very ugly.) So my mom asks again, "What's wrong with my son?" My retarded-ass cousin says, "Nothin', see?" and decides to turn a blind eye to the fact that I can't walk. He lets go of me and I crash into the china cabinet. And you know how black women feel about those china cabinets! Especially one with thirteen snow globes in it. Then he goes into his show business, talkin' about "Yeah, see what had happened was, Hadjii and myself were hangin' out. We split up momentarily, as in I was nowhere near him so there's no need to call my parents, so anyway I found him, and apparently someone, I have no idea who, but someone must have put some stuff in his drink or something and now he's sick. Well anyway, I gotta go."

Somehow I made it to my room before passing out, and I woke up the next morning with this strange feeling, thinking, "Damn . . . What a fucked-up nightmare." Then I touched my neck and realized that I still had all my fresh-to-death chains on. Then I realized that I was still wearing my fresh-to-death shirt. I'm still wearing my jeans. Then I clicked my feet together and noticed that I still had my fuckin' shoes on! And I was under the covers! You mean it wasn't a dream? Aww damn. By the way, whose fuckin' jeans are these?

Now came the real moment of truth, because before I thought about the damage that I had done to homeboy's sink, before I thought about how bad I smelled, and how much my head was hurting, there was only one thought running through my mind. I've gotta face Daddy.

Then I got up and I noticed that my mom wasn't home, which let me know how fucked up this shit really was, cause usually, as all brothas know, when you and ya pops really have it out, your mom's the one who doesn't let things get too out of hand. Sometimes mothers have to actually stand in between y'all to keep that nigga from killin' you for real. But I guess she didn't wanna stick around for this one. And I hadn't had a beatin' since I was like nine or ten years old. But that's not to say he hadn't hit me since then. The older you get, the higher the blows get. When you're a baby you get a pop on the legs. When you're five through twelve or whatever, they hit'cha on ya butt, maybe with their hand or maybe with a belt, or for all you extremists out there, spiked paddles and folding chairs. Y'all know the routine. However, now I'm fifteen and comin' home drunk? This is like a pretty manly fuck-up. Like, he might treat me like a man or somethin' and knock a tooth out. I mean, y'all know how excited he gets at the thought of loose teeth. And my "Love me tender / Love me true" mama ain't even here to stop it. And I'm like, "Damn, first the Boogie Man. Now my mama? Who can I trust 'round this mufucka?"

So I get my game plan down and walk into the kitchen and was instantly thrown for a loop, because my pops threw me an absolute curveball. I mean, he was watching CNN or some news channel as expected, but he was sittin' on the sofa? He wasn't in his chair. He was on the sofa. Needless to say, I wasn't prepared for this. Should I just go back to my room and regroup or go ahead and get this over with? Maybe wait until MY MOM gets home. Aww, fuck it. I'm fifteen. I'm a man. Let's go.

So I walk into the den and we sit there in silence. Actually, he was sitting. I made sure I was on my feet just in case, well, ya know. So we're like this for about five minutes with him momentarily giving me that cold-ass glare of his off and on. (Parents: Whenever you wanna scare the shit out of a kid, use silence. Unless you can get some of that *Friday the 13th* Jason "Shee-shee-hah-ha" music to accompany you.) So we just sit there for another five or ten minutes and the silence is killin' me, and that's when it hit me. My mom was one of the most cunning and downright devious people I'll ever encounter, cause she set it up in such a way that I can't tell whether or not she told him what happened. The nerve. So we're just sitting there, and I'm trying to feel him out, but there was only one problem. There is no feeling my pops out. He was serious all the time. There is no good or bad mood. There's bad mood and very bad mood. But I'm a gambler, got damn it. Game on.

So I'm standing there and now the wheels are turnin' in my mind because I'm trying to figure out how I wanna play this. If I ask, "Did you talk to Mama?" or "Did she tell you about last night?," etc., and she didn't, I just played myself. Cause then he's gonna ask, "What do I need to know about last night?" and the shit's just gonna go downhill from there. However, here's where it gets tricky, because if she did tell him about last night, maybe this is one of those moments where he's waiting on me to step up to the plate, fess up, and take it like a man. And maybe he's gonna make me stand here with him in complete silence until I do that. That sounds like somethin' he'd do. Like I said, this was a manly fuck-up. This is a man moment. A little more time passes and by now, I'm really thinkin' Plan B's the move, because it's kinda like when ya get caught cheating in a relationship. You know you've been caught, but at least if you fess up you can salvage some of those at-least-I-told-the-truth points. Okay, here goes nothin', and right before I said, "Daddy," I thought, Wait! Plan C! I'ma force this nigga's hand! What I'ma do is turn and begin to walk out of the room like I've got somewhere to go or somethin' to do. If she told him, he'll stop me. If I get outta this room, he doesn't know.

So I began to walk out and I felt his voice, yes felt his voice crawl up my back as he said, "Hadjii. Come back in here and sit down for a minute." Aww shit. And what really messed me up even more was that he motioned for me to sit in his chair. This shit was so weird that by now I was waiting for Alfred Hitchcock or that *Twilight Zone* nigga to come out of the bathroom and explain to the audience what was about to happen. But neither one of 'em showed up.

So I sit there and he's putting his clipboard and the little stuff he was drawing to the side. Then finally, he looks at me and says, "Hadjii, we need to talk." Aww double-shit. Everybody knows that when somebody says, "We need to talk" or "Can I talk to you?" something bad is about to happen. So when my pops said, "We need to talk," I'm like, "Okay, just knock out one of the back teeth cause I don't really need those that much." I've got dimples, and dimples are like magic, but dimples without one of your front teeth? That's like being an ugly nigga with good hair. What's the fuckin' point?

My pops was like, "Sit down for a minute and lemme talk to you." "Okay, some bonding time between a father and son is a good thing," I replied. " . . . . ," he said. "Fuck," I thought.

"You're getting older now, and I know you're getting the desire to try new things, and I wanna make sure you're doing things right." And I'm thinking, "Okay, this is cool. He's about to give me a bottle of Scotch." And then the strangest thing in the world happened. He reaches over and grabs this little bag he had sitting on the floor and hands it to me. I slowly reach over, grab the bag, check it to make sure it isn't ticking, open it, and guess what's inside? Condoms. Condoms? Condoms! You had me sittin' in here about to piss all over myself over some got damn condoms?

"Ya need to use these to prevent you from catching AIDS or any other sexually transmitted diseases alright. Now look at the package. You wanna make sure you use the ones that have that 'Nonoxynal-9' on 'em cause that's what kills the AIDS virus." "Yes sir, Daddy! Well, I gotta go to my room and practice! Holla!"

About thirty minutes later, my mom came home and barged into my room. Soon as she opened the door I said, "Mama, thank you so much for not tellin' Daddy about—" and she cut me off like, "Yeah, yeah whatever, nigga. Did your daddy give you a bag of condoms?" "Yes," I replied. "Where are they?" she demanded. "Right here." And then she starts snapping her finger at me like "Hand'em here! Give'em to me!" and it's taking me a minute to give'em to her because, number one, I didn't want to. I mean after all, these are my condoms and I had big plans for these suckas, and number two, handin' ya mom a bag of condoms has gotta be some of the most awkward shit in the world. I'm fumblin' around and have condoms fallin' out all over the place and shit and then she just snatched'em from me and said, "You won't be needing these, cause I don't support no poo-tang before marriage in my house! Ain't no boinkin' 'round here without a license!" and walked out, with my condoms. No condoms. No whiskey. But hey, I've still got my teeth. But where in the hell did I get these jeans from?

A Little AIDS
Ain't Never Hurt Nobody!

Ya know how there are those times in your life, usually tragedies, that take place and years later you can still remember exactly where you were and what you were doing when you heard the news? Like, I was standing in line at one of those quick-cash places waiting to pay my phone bill when my mom called me on my cellphone to tell me my father had died. Or one morning, I woke up and took my comforter into the living room to lay on the couch for another hour and watch *Jenny Jones* before I started my day. I turn on the television and see footage of a plane flying into a building. I had no idea that day was gonna become 9/11. Then there's Columbine, Tupac and Biggie dying, O.J. rolling down the freeway messing up the Knicks and Rockets game, Bill Cosby's son getting murdered, and the list goes on and on. Including the day Magic Johnson announced he was HIV positive.

Remember when Magic Johnson announced he was HIV positive and everybody thought he was gonna die next week? Matter of fact, I even remember watching this so-called expert talk about how America was gonna watch as "this great man shriveled up and died right before our eyes." Can you believe she actually said that? Now, like fifteen years later, he's probably healthier than the average twenty-five-year-old. He's definitely got me beat. Go 'head witcha bad self. I mean, dude has given hope to everybody.

Anyway, I was in high school at the time, and all the sudden you couldn't go anywhere without somebody giving you a pamphlet about AIDS and the HIV virus. People would come to our school and set up booths in the cafeteria and ask ya if you were gettin' any yet and do you know how to use a condom. Then they'd give you some pamphlets and some condoms and send you on your merry way. "Here's a rubber to go with that ice cream. Here, practice on this banana." Health counselors would interrupt Math class and ask us if we were gettin' any yet and did we know how to use a condom and say, "Here's some rubbers and some cucumbers to practice with." People would pull our school bus over and ask everybody if we were gettin' any yet and did we know how to use condoms. "Here, practice on the bus driver." But as they say in the good ole U.S. of A., "Time heals all wounds," and once the initial shock of Magic's announcement passed over, people were back to boinkin' like never before, and it makes ya wonder, ya know? I mean, between *Girls Gone Wild*, MTV *Spring Break*, *Wild on E!*, the now deceased sexfest better known as Freaknik, the porn industry, penis-enhancing drugs, breast enlargements, hedonism, *elimiDATE*, swing parties, escort services, prostitution, Steve Urkel sex tapes, and on and on and on, doesn't it make ya think damn near everybody in the world should have that there virus by now? Because the world's love for sex hasn't slowed down a bit.

It's easy to forget it, but the threat is way too real. Matter of fact, back in the day when you were dating a woman and things were starting to get serious you used to be afraid that one night y'all would be having a romantic evening and then the next thing ya know, she was gonna hit'chou with those four terrifying words, "Do you love me?" Now those four words have been replaced with the hellafied fear of a new four words that are way scarier than those: "You ever been tested?" And as men, we all give that same rehearsed answer, "Well, ya know, I've had some bloodwork done before but—" And all the fellas know by now that the ladies ain't fallin' for that one anymore. They're like, "No. I mean have you ever been tested? Taken the test? Specifically asked for an

AIDS test? Have you been to the clinic? Can I see some paperwork? Some documentation?" And I'm not talkin' about some girl you're just havin' a good time with. I'm talkin' about the woman you feel is The One. You love'er, right? And you know she's making sense, and you know that you really do need to know, but as a man you also feel like, and forgive my French, "Shiiiitt, if I got it? Fuck it. I don't wanna know." Cause doesn't it seem like people who have it and don't know it are just chillin' and having a good time and everything's fine? Then they go and test positive for it and all the sudden they lose like a hundred pounds the next week? Maybe ignorance *is* bliss.

But at the same time fear is killing you! Know why? Cause if you've never been tested that fear sets up shop in your brain! You can't focus on anything without the thought, "Do I have that shit?" poppin' up in your mind at least eighty-five times a day. You could be sitting there about to eat lunch. Say your grace, "God, thank you for this food we're about to receive. Let it be healthy and nourishing to our bodies. Amen. And by the way, God, if ya don't mind. Please don't let me have AIDS." Add to that the fact that women always hit'cha with that line, "Ya know, even if you do test positive, nothing will change between us. I won't leave you, because I love you." And you're thinking to yourself, "*Ewww. Nasty.*" Then they even take it a step further and really pull your punk card when they say, "I'll even go and get tested with you. We can do it together." Checkmate, match, and game point. You might as well go ahead and warm up the car, because you're going to get tested, buddy.

Then two things happen. Number one, you realize that she's never gonna let you boink her until you get some paperwork, and number two, you start doing everything earthly possible you can do to diagnose yourself *outside* of getting tested. And anybody who knows me knows that I'm paranoid. I'm so 'noided I put condoms on pay phones. Ain't no tellin' who was the last person to use it. I even used to take before-and-after pictures of myself before I had sex and compare 'em a week later, cause if I saw a new bump or scar on myself I was gonna kill somebody. Have you ever gotten a new bump and then spent the rest of the day trying to remember whether it's new or not? "Was this hairy eyeball on my penis a month ago? Oh yeah, it's always been there. Cause I remember one time I was havin' sex with this ugly chick and my dick kept its eye closed. I'm fine." Then you make the biggest mistake a person afraid of their status can ever make. You took your dumb ass over to the library or got on the Internet and looked up the symptoms. Every time I see a thugged-out brotha in the library on a computer I look at 'em and say, "Ya dick ain't feelin' right, huh?"

See, the mind is a trip, and if you're afraid that you might have a condition, don't look up the symptoms, because you are going to have every single one of 'em. "Light-headedness, nausea, cravings, swollen glands, enlarged belly." Oh my God! I'm the world's first pregnant man! The world's first pregnant man with an eye on his dick. "Damn it! I knew something wasn't right when I missed my period."

So you go to the clinic. Not the one everybody else goes to, but the one on the other side of town (like the one in Wyoming), and the clinic can be a cold and cruel place. First of all, you go in there expecting to take an anonymous AIDS test. News flash: ain't a damn thang anonymous about no hospital, no clinic, no checkup, no visit, no nothing. Matter of fact, the first thing they do soon as you walk in the door is ask you ya damn name. Then, no matter if you're the only person in the entire clinic, they make you wait four hours to see the doctor. You know how many thoughts can run through your mind in four hours? One! "What the fuck am I doing here?" And you start thinking, "I'll just tell the ole lady that they were taking too long here at the clinic and I had to get back to work. I'll come back another day when I've got more time, like next year or somethin'." And right as you get up and begin to head for the door a nurse enters and says, "The doctor will see you now."

So you go to the back and get escorted to a room, and another person besides the doctor, usually a woman from your church, starts getting all in your business.

NURSE: Why are you here?
ME: I want an STD screening.
NURSE: There's no such thing as an STD screening.
ME: But that's what that lady told me during lunch in tenth grade.

NURSE: I'm sorry, Mr. Hand, but there's no such
thing as an STD screening. You gotta pick one. You
wanna be tested for herpes, genital warts,
gonorrhea, what?

ME: (whisper) Can I take an AIDS test, please?

NURSE: Excuse me?

ME: (whisper) AIDS.

NURSE: I can't hear you.

ME: AIDS!

NURSE: Don't get mad at me cause you scared! Now,
why do you want an AIDS test? Don't you practice
safe sex? Do you know how to properly use a
condom? Do I need to bring some bananas in
here?

ME: No, I don't want no fuckin' banana.

NURSE: Then why are you here?

ME: Because y'all said on the commercial that
everybody needs to be tested. Why you makin' me
feel insecure?

NURSE: Okay, so are you experiencing any weight
loss, dry cough, scaly skin, night sweats, or dick
drip?

ME: Where's the doctor?

NURSE: Again, are you experiencing any weight loss,
dry cough, scaly skin, night sweats, or dick drip?

ME: No.

NURSE: So why are you so antsy?

ME: Because I've been experiencing weight loss, dry
cough, scaly skin, night sweats, and dick drip, ya
nosy bitch. Now where's the doctor?

NURSE: So you wanna take an AIDS test?

ME: Yes!

NURSE: Okay. The doctor will be in to see you
soon . . .

Two hours later. The doctor finally enters.

DOCTOR: How ya doing?

ME: How am I doing? I don't know. I guess I'm about
as happy as a nigga who thinks he might have
AIDS can be. Can I get my test on, please?

DOCTOR: Have you been experiencing any weight
loss, dry cough, scaly skin, night sweats, or dick
drip?

ME: What? You been talkin' to that nurse or
somethin'?

DOCTOR: No. By the way, why are you naked? I just
need a blood sample.

ME: Oh? My bad.

And a lot of strange things happen to you once you
take an AIDS test. Number one, you realize that the
Bible's a really good book. Number two, you begin to rationalize why it's fair if you do have it, because you start
to reflect on all the evil things you've done to people in
the past. "I knew I shouldn't've cheated off that girl in
Science class in the seventh grade. I got AIDS. I told that
Salvation Army dude I ain't have no money knowing I
had twenty dollars in my pocket. Yep, I got AIDS."

Then you start treatin' your girlfriend extra nice, so

that just in case you test positive, she won't leave you. So now you start lettin' all kinds of bullshit slide. You mean you didn't spend Valentine's Day with me cause you were having sex with your ex-boyfriend? Aww, don't worry about it. I'm a forgiving person. And I know you'd forgive me if I ever did some off-the-wall shit like forget to tape the soaps for you, or didn't bring you a present on your birthday, or I don't know, gave you a terminal illness, for example. You would forgive me, wouldn't ya? Never know when ya gonna have to forgive a nigga . . . By the way, have you been experiencin' any dick drip lately?

Then it seems like every TV show, commercial, song, public service announcement, you name it, is about Living with the HIV Virus or Getting Tested. Turn to Maury, "So he was positive and didn't tell you?" Turn to MTV, "Get tested now!" Turn on the radio, "Come support AIDS Awareness Day." Then you've got those radio spots, "Do you know that before this thirty-second spot is finished over thirty thousand people in America will have contracted the HIV/AIDS virus?" And I'd be like, "Then y'all need to stop runnin' this fuckin' commercial. Obviously there must be some type of connection." Then you see those dumb commercials for shit like herpes and genital warts. Are you kiddin' me? They'll say something like, "We can help you with your herpes. By the way, this product may not be safe for those who have HIV or Acquired Immune Deficiency Syndrome." And I'm like, what? If you got AIDS who gives a fuck about a little herpes? I mean you've got bigger fish to fry. Shit, I'd trade in my AIDS for some herpes any day. I'd even star in one of them commercials myself. It'd be me and my horse playin' Scrabble on the beach or some shit all her-peed up. I wouldn't care. But the worst commercials are the ones that trick you before you get a chance to turn the channel. Like it'll be a beautiful woman jogging down the beach in a little tiny dental-floss bikini and she'll be playing Frisbee with her dog while her hair's flowing in the wind and her boobs are bouncing up and down, and then she'll say, "You woulda never thought I was HIV positive, would you?"

Then it gets even worse, because it makes you start thinking about all the women you've ever been with. And there's always that one girl from your past that was just a tad too much fun to not have nothin'. Then you begin to blame her for all this shit. "I can't believe that nasty chick dragged me to all those freaky-deaky orgies and forced me to drink all that free liquor and have unpro-tected sex with all those Brazilian strippers for three years. How could she do that to me?"

So what do you do when all is lost and there's nowhere else to turn? You pray. You pray and you pray hard, and when you're done praying, you pray some more. "God, it's me again. Look, I know I wasn't thinkin' about you much when I was drinking all that free liquor and having unprotected sex with all those Brazilian strip-pers, but if you let me test negative, I promise I will be your friend. Please don't do me like the Boogie Man and my mama did. Amen."

Cause by now, not only are you afraid of having it because of the health effects, but then you start thinking about everybody else. If I've got it, I've gotta tell my mama. Oh fuck me. Then she's gonna tell my daddy. Oh double fuck me! Cause in the movies a family'll be at dinner, ya know? Chillin', and then the dude'll say, "We need to talk." (Didn't I tell y'all about that "We need to talk" line earlier?) And it'll play out something like this . . .

WHITE SON: We need to talk.

DADDY: What's on your mind?

SON: Well, I'm HIV positive.

MOM: Oh my God, no.

DADDY: How can this be? I mean there must be
    some mistake. After all, you're white and studies
    show this type of thing doesn't happen to us.

SON: I know.

DADDY: I mean it's not like we live in a trailer park
    or something. Then this might make sense, but this
    is ridiculous. You sure you didn't go to some
    foreign doctor with a personal vendetta?

SON: No. I've got it.

MOM: Well that's okay, son. We're gonna weather
    this storm together, because we're a family and we
    love you.

Then there's like a big group hug and they go on to continue with business as usual and fight that thang together. Black families are a little different. I mean, don't get me wrong. We'll stick together, but that's a conclusion that we come to eventually. The initial response goes a little something like this:

BLACK SON: I need to talk to y'all.

DADDY: Got damn it. You done fucked up ya rent money again, didn't ya? Ya know a real man can pay for shit on his own.

SON: No. I've got money. But I'm HIV positive.

MAMA: Oh sweet Lawd, Doctor Jesus on high have mercy on me! First crusty draws, now this. Please, King Jesus, wake me up when you're ready, cause I'm about to pass out.

DADDY: You got *what*, boy?

BLACK SON: I—

DADDY: You mean you ain't been usin' them rubbers I gave ya?

BLACK SON: Mama took'em from me . . .

MAMA: Oh don't blame this on me. That was fifteen years ago. Now y'all put this food away. We about to fast and pray that AIDS up outta you, boy. Go in my bedroom and bring me my Bible, some oil, and my Mississippi Mass Choir tape. Hurry up 'fore that AIDS sets in.

Then the news travels through the family via telephone.

AUNT 1: Well, I knew something was fishy when he didn't want any of my potato salad that time, cause

everybody loves my potato salad, and if you don't
want none of my potato salad something just ain't
right.

AUNT 2: And ya know he used to always have that
music up so loud. That's a sign too. That AIDS give
ya impaired hearing. And wearin' them big ole
baggy jeans. That's impaired judgment. That's
another symptom.

AUNT 1: Umm-hmm. Well I told you about the time
he was at my house and that book of matches fell
out his pocket? I didn't tell you about that? Guurrl,
he was at my house one time and a book of
matches fell out his pocket! You know what that
mean, dontcha? Means he's smokin' crack too. Wait
a minute. I got a beep on the other line. Hello.

AUNT 3: Y'all heard the news?

AUNT 1: Guuurrrlll, we talkin' 'bout it now.

AUNT 3: I knew somethin' was up when he wouldn't
eat none of my banana puddin'.

AUNT 1: He wouldn't eat my potato salad either! The
boy is sick, I tell ya. But lemme call you back. I'm
watchin' *Prison Break*.

Now here come your uncles, and your uncles handle
situations a little differently. See, middle-aged black men
whether they know it or not are ten times worse than
women when it comes to being nosy, cause they've gotta
understand everything. They'll sit there and drag an ex-
planation outta ya until you put it in terms where they
can understand.

UNCLE: Boy, sit down. Lemme talk to ya. Now rumor
has it you done went out there and caught that
virus?

NEPHEW: Yeah.

UNCLE: I didn't know you were gay.

NEPHEW: I'm not.

UNCLE: You sure?

NEPHEW: Yeah.

UNCLE: So you got a drug habit or somethin'?

NEPHEW: Nah.

UNCLE: Porn star?

NEPHEW: No!

UNCLE: Hey, don't get mad at me. I ain't the one
gave ya the shit. I'm just concerned about 'cha
welfare, nigga. If you ain't ready to talk about it I
understand. I'll give ya ya space. I'm just
concerned, and I'm here for ya. You don't wanna
talk about it, we ain't gotta talk about it.

NEPHEW: Thanks.

UNCLE: So how'd ya get it?

NEPHEW: I don't know.

UNCLE: You don't know? Whatcha mean ya don't
know? AIDS don't just fall outta the sky?!   .
(concerned) Does it?

NEPHEW: No.

UNCLE: So you ain't ask the doctor or nothin'?
Aintcha curious? Investigate, mufucka. Ask
around. Go on line. Now, is ya insurance gonna
cover this or what? Cause these last few weeks I

been experiencin' some swellin' in my left knee. Ya
don't think I got it, do ya? I mean after all, we have
been smokin' a lot of weed together and you do
have a tendency to leave the blunt pretty wet
witcha saliva. I'd hate to have to kill you, boy.

Then, as if that weren't enough, you gotta tell her
mama and daddy. And then shit's really gonna escalate
when they tell her crazy-ass uncles, because every fine
black woman has got at least two violent-ass uncles. It's
part of the package. They even pay the "crazy, nothing to
lose" uncle's bail money so he can get outta jail for a
week and make sure things are done properly. "That ain't
how ya puncture a lung. Y'all don't know nothin'.
Gimme that pipe."

Damn, I shoulda stayed a virgin like my mom told me
to. Okay, God, ya got me. I'm pretty scared right now. I
need your love, I need your grace, I need your kindness,
and your mercy. Forget about cars, clothes, and all that
other unnecessary crap. Just give me a clean test, and I'll
work at Captain D's for the rest of my life. I'll be the
happiest shrimp and hushpuppies droppin' muthafucka
you've ever seen. Just let me be negative."

Because not only do you have to worry about all of the
things I mentioned above, but you also have to deal with
the final frontier, which is your friends finding out and
spreading the news. Now this is difficult for anybody, but
it's especially hard for black men, cause black men ain't
too good at handlin' bad news. You'd think we'd be used

to it, but in actuality we can't even talk about it, and we especially suck at delivering bad news.

First of all, we can't stand still. When young black men are delivering bad news, walking, pacing, rocking, and swaying become mandatory. And the worse the news the longer the walk. One time I came home from school and my dad was sitting on the front porch and said, "Have a seat, Hadjii. I've got somethin' to tell you." And then he just walked off. Came back three hours later and said, "Your dog died." I remember one time he called me in the living room and said, "Hadjii . . ." and I ain't see that nigga again for like five weeks. Then he came back home seventy pounds lighter and said, "Did you know Vanessa Williams was married?" And please don't ever try to get some bad news out of a young cat. Have you ever had a twenty-one-year-old brotha try to break some bad news to you? That shit takes seventy-nine hours. Cause seventy-eight hours and forty-five minutes are spent on buildup and pronouns.

BROTHA 1: What's up, man?
BROTHA 2: Nothin'.
BROTHA 1: (sighs) *Wooooh.*

And they've gotta shake their head "no" the entire time. It helps them think.

BROTHA 1 (continues): Man. Shawty.
BROTHA 2: What?

BROTHA 1: You heard about'cha boy?

BROTHA 2: Who?

BROTHA 1: You know who.

BROTHA 2: Nah. Who?

BROTHA 1: Oh you ain't heard? Cuz. (sighs) You know we boys, right? So I ain't told this shit to nobody else.

BROTHA 2: You ain't told me yet either, nigga. Spit it out. I'm getting motion sickness.

BROTHA 1: (sighs) Buddy.

BROTHA 2: What?

BROTHA 1: Playa. (sighs) Homie. (sighs) My nigga, ya boy done fucked up.

BROTHA 2: Who?

BROTHA 1: I don't even wanna talk about it.

Then the moment of reckoning comes. Ya know they have the nerve to tell you stuff like, "Come up here around two o'clock. We'll have your results by then." Two o'clock? It's only nine-fifteen. What am I supposed to do until two? That's why every employer should give you a day of vacation time called Results Day, cause you can't focus on a damn thing at work when you got that looming over ya head. I mean the monthly report ain't high on my list of priorities right now. Can't'chou see it's nine-seventeen? Then two o'clock finally decides to show up. Of course, you've been sitting in the clinic parking lot since eleven-thirty, but never mind that. You've got two reactions planned. One for if you're positive, cause you don't wanna overreact. Then one for negative, cause you don't wanna act too surprised or else the doctor might ask you to take the test again. And as you're sitting there in absolute fear and distress trying to squeeze a few more last-second prayers in, you begin to hear a piercing, shrieking nuisance that is the last thing anyone in the world wants to hear at a time like this. It's that fifteen-year-old bitch with the cellphone sittin' behind you!

One of those girls usually wearing about five gold necklaces, seventeen bracelets, a couple of rings per hand with long fingernails, a bad hair weave, one of those velvet jogging suits with a word like *JUICY* written across the ass, and the letters are usually going up her crack so it looks more like *J/Y*, and she's on her cellphone having an important conversation.

"Guurrrl, no she didn't. No she didn't! I wish I was dere right now cuz I'll tell'er about herself, but I'm up at the clinic cuz the doctor say he think my baby got an ear infection, but whateva. I tried to tell'em his ear look like dat all da time.

"But anyway, dat bitch need to check herself 'fore she come tryin' to say somethin' 'bout me. Okay? Cause Tawangelisha ain't the one. I will cuss dat bitch smooth da fuck out and not think nothin' of it. Okay? She don't know nuttin' 'bout me. What she need to do is take dat ole fake-ass Gucci bag she be carryin' 'round and throw that shit in the Mexican Ocean, okay. She jus' mad cause she had seen me wit' her baby-daddy at da mall dis weekend. No, not dat baby-daddy, her other baby-daddy. Da fine one. Dennnn, later dat night, she had seented us again up in da Waffle House eatin' for free cause he got da hook-up cause he work dere. Shoot yeah, gurl. I had got me da grilled chicken wit' da hash browns scattered, smothered, and chunked. We was doin' it big, guurrrlll.

"Oh! And guess whut, guuurrrll? Guess who had da nerve to come up in dere and call hisself havin' an attitude wit' me? Tyreke. Yes! Umm-hmm. That's what I said, girl. He gonna call me da next day talkin' 'bout, 'Who was dat nigga I seentch you in da Waffle House wit'?' and I was like, 'First of all, don't even be comin' at me like dat. You ain't my man. If you cared so much about me, why you ain't come to my birfday party?' Wasn't my birfday party off da chain, guuurrllll? Gurrl, we had so much fun. I don't know whut Ray-Ray call hisself doin' out dere on da dance flo. I told him, 'Ray-Ray, you dance like a white boy!' [Bursts into laughter.] But he is kinda cute, ain't he? Wit' his little cute self. I would get wit' him, but he still live in his mama house and you know I ain't got time for that. Shoot, I'm fifteen years old.

"Plus his mama be actin' all like she don't like me and stuff. Talkin' 'bout she thank I'm ghetto cause my name Tawangelisha, but white girls be named Navanarolla and Kourinakash and don't nobody thank they ghetto. Plus she don't think I'm right for him cause he thirty-two and I'm fifteen, but I'm like, "Whateva. Whateva. It ain't all 'bout da birf certificate. It's 'bout what I'm workin' wit.

"Shoot, wait a minute, gurl. I got a beep. Hello? Who

is dis? Tyreke, wait. Umm, slow down. See, you be—. Umm-umm, see, dat's why I can't even—. Hold on, Tyreke. Gurll, dis Tyreke on da other line. Lemme call you back. Hello? See, dere you go. Tyreke, I told you we was jus' friends. Dat's my friend. Well, I don't care what'cho boys been tellin' you. Yo boys is lyin' to you. Anyway, I ain't da one dat was all up in English class all hugged up on Swanzetta, am I? Wait? Was dat me? Was dat me? No! Dat was you! . . . Oh for real? . . . You was jus' tryin' to make me jealous? Tyreke, you so silly! . . . What am I wearin'? Tyreke, I'm on da clinic, fool. I can't be tellin' you all dat . . . Well, I'm wearin' my pink velvet joggin' suit dat say *JUICY* on da back . . . Yes, I got on da thongs. Are you happy now? No, I can't come over dere. I got homework . . . Yo mama at choir practice? . . . Whut church yo mama go to? . . . Ooh, ask'er do she know my auntie? She go there too . . . Umm-hmm. She a percussionist.

"Whut? Tyreke, hold up. I got a beep . . . Hello? . . . Hey Ray-Ray. Hold on a minute. I got somebody on da other line. Hold on. Tyreke? I'll call you back . . . Hello? . . . Ray-Ray, no I wasn't talkin' to no man. Dat was my girlfriend. She want me to go to da doctor wit' her tomorrow cause they think her baby got an ear infection, but she said her baby ear be like that all the time . . . See, Ray-Ray, dat's yo problem. You always talkin' 'bout wantin' to kill somebody. Me and Tyreke is over. Why you so insecure? . . . Well, I don't care what'cho boys been tellin' you. Yo boys is lyin' to you . . . So you gonna shoot every man you see me talkin' to? . . . Well, have it'cho way . . . I ain't even got time for dis. I gotta go . . . Cause you talkin' crazy . . . Yeah, I love you too, Ray-Ray, but still . . . Da Bible say, 'Dou shalt not kill.' Aintcha never read da Bible? . . . I don't wanna be comin' to prison to see you again . . .

"Hold up. I got a beep. Hello? . . . Tyreke, I told you I was gonna call you back . . . Yes, I'm talkin' to Ray-Ray, but I'ma call you back . . . Tyreke, you know I wanna marry you soon as I finish tenf grade! Why you trippin'?"

And right before I get up to either leave or strangle this bitch, a nurse walks in and says, "Mr. Hand, we're ready for you now." Damn.

"To make a long story short, you're negative." Whoopie!

"First thing I'ma do is go home and see if my old lady'll stop makin' me wear them condoms!"

Just jivin'. Just jivin'.

"Hadjii . . . Da Man Will See You Now"

Remember when you got your first real job? I mean your first *real job*. The one where you were finally putting that college degree to use. I'm talking résumés and cover letters, letters of recommendation, references, interviews, job fairs, and rejection. The first job you ever had without a time clock. The first job that didn't come with a uniform. You had a set schedule. Staff meetings, yearly evaluations, vacation time, insurance, and sick days. Sick days? Wait. Lemme get this straight, you mean if I call into work, and say I can't come in cause I'm not feelin' good, I still get paid? I think I feel a little leprosy comin' on.

I hated the whole process. First of all, ya go to school, ya get an internship, ya try to be a good person and help old ladies cross the street and all that other dumb shit cause you're workin' on your karma points. Right? Then ya spend thousands upon thousands of dollars to buy you one of them edumacations, only to find yourself one day staring blankly at a computer screen looking for jobs, and that's when it hits you. "Damn, I spent all that money on college yet I still ain't qualified to do a got damn thang. Who do these people think they are with all these demands? What do I need experience for? And how the hell am I supposed to get some experience if nobody'll give me a fuckin' job?" Then ya finally find a few that you might have a crack at, so now you've gotta come up with a résumé. That's when ya really realize that ninety percent of all the things you've done in your life are pretty fuckin' insignificant. So who do you turn to when you need to make a bunch of bullshit look good? Ya call a woman. Ya know how women can come over to your little junky-ass apartment and throw a couple of pictures on the wall and a rug on the floor and all the sudden your place is livable? Well they can do that with your résumé too. Cause women are good at fakin' it. Especially my woman. Wait a minute, you don't think she . . . ? Anyway, a woman can take your life and experiences and make them sound so much more impressive than they really are. My lady'll sit there with me and say, "Now what have you done?"

"With what?"

"With your life."

"Oh well, lemme see, when I was in high school I worked at a record store once."

"Experience in promotion, soliciting funds, and artist management. What else ya got?"

"Uhh, one time I had a job at a public pool where I was in charge of keeping all the kids' shoes and house keys together."

"Supervised and oversaw all assets in real estate."

Then you give all this bullshit to some employer and they actually buy it, and call you in for an interview. That's when the lies really start to fly, cause they ask ya a bunch of stupid questions you have to answer as best as possible.

EMPLOYER: So, why do you want to work here?

ME: Well, ever since I can remember I've followed your organization very closely, and I believe deeply in what you guys stand for and what you represent, and the work that you do in the community, and I'm very excited about the possibility of joining this team and learning and enhancing my life.

EMPLOYER: Excellent. So how familiar are you with our services?

ME: I'm probably as familiar as one can be without having actually been employed here. For years you guys have been providing several services to the community with programs that aid, support, and

educate. I know you also have social programs,
promotions, and other means of marketing. Umm,
you guys are pretty much the heartbeat of this
entire city.

EMPLOYER: How do you feel you would fit in here?

ME: Gee whiz. Most people think of me as a people
person, but really and truly I feel that I'm more
than that. I'm a team player. I'm a good leader, but
I also know how to follow and I'm willing to do
whatever it takes to help this team win. Did I
mention my energy?

EMPLOYER: Do you have any questions for me?

ME: No. You've been more than informative in every
way.

Now was that a bunch of bullshit or what? The truth
won't get you too far in a job interview. Could you imagine me givin' the real answers to those questions?

EMPLOYER: So, why do you want to work here?

ME: I don't. I don't wanna work no fuckin' place. I
mean let's face it, I'll never get rich workin' for
y'all. I'm just helpin' y'all get rich. In all honesty I
guess I wanna work here cause I gotta pay a bunch
of bills. Plus I'm tired to tellin' women I still live
with my mama.

EMPLOYER: Excellent. So how familiar are you with
our services?

ME: Well, to be perfectly honest, I'd never even heard

of y'all muthafuckas until Gladys, ya know the black lady who works here, told my mama y'all was hirin'.

EMPLOYER: Why do you feel you would be a good fit here?

ME: Cause I don't care enough to cause any trouble. Trust me. If you hire me I promise you that I will not cause any waves, not even one got damn ripple, cause I don't care. Staff meetings, I ain't got shit to say. I have no opinions or suggestions. No bright ideas. I have absolutely nothing to contribute nor do I have or will I ever develop any type of emotional attachment to this job, this company, or you. So if you tell me to do something I don't agree with, I'm not gonna cause any commotions or anything like that. I'm just gonna say, "I'm on it." And then I'ma wait until somebody else does it, cause that what teammates are for.

EMPLOYER: Do you have any questions for me?

ME: Uhh, let me see. How much does this job pay? How many vacation days do we get? What about sick days? Comp time? Overtime? How much does this job pay? Weekends off? We do get MLK Day, don't we? Do I really have to be here at nine and stay all the way until five or is that just some employment slang? Raises? Why did the person I'm replacin' leave? How much does this job pay? Health insurance? Dental? Vision? IRA? 401(k)? Company car? Can a nigga at least get a cellphone?

A pager? Company mug? Oh yeah, how long is
lunch? How much does this job pay? And uhh, do
y'all drug-test?

Then on top of all that they've got the nerve to make
all these demands before they even hire you. They wanna
know if you're gonna be on time every day, and what
your future plans are, and the question that really gets
me is, "Can you type more than seventy-five words a
minute?" Seventy-five words a minute? Shit, nigga. It's
sixty minutes in an hour. Twenty-four hours in a day.
What the fuck I need to type seventy-five words a minute
for? I ain't even got that much shit to say. You want me
to type 108,000 words a day? This is some bullshit. I
quit. "But you haven't even been hired yet." Told you I
was ambitious.

Then, much to your dismay they actually hire you, and
it's a trip, because your first real job is kind of cool at
first. Then of course the newness wears off as all things
do. That's why I used to bug out whenever I saw that one
guy or that one lady who's like really into their job. Ya
know that person who's always the first one there and the
last one to leave? I used to wonder like, Okay, I know
they ain't makin' that much money here to be so dedi-
cated. Their job isn't that time-consuming.

Then I figured it out. The one cool thing about havin'
a real job is that at least it gives you a life away from home,
because sitting at home all day ain't nothing but a recipe
for insanity. You've gotta have a life away from home. I

think it's even more necessary for women, because they actually get to be around people they don't have to take care of for a change. I remember after a hard day's work my mom would come home and as soon as she'd walk inside I'd say, "Hey Mama, I got a pack of pork chops thawing in the sink." Now what kinda rude shit is that? You don't talk to no woman like that. But then again, she ain't no woman. That's my mama. And for men, sometimes ya just need a break from ya ole lady. Sometimes ya just wanna go somewhere and "be somewhere." And if I gotta go dig ditches to get that feeling of being somewhere? Pass the shovel.

Plus the workplace can be very refreshing in its own way. Like sometimes my woman'll come home and say, "I got so many compliments at work today, and this one old man said I looked good. He even asked me if I had been workin' out because he said it looked like I had lost some weight and my legs were gettin' more toned." And I'll be thinkin', "Damn. How'd I miss all that? Ya look the same to me. Anyway, I got a pack of pork chops thawing in the sink." And it works the same way for me, because my girl doesn't find me sexy anymore. Can you imagine that? I don't even think she loves me anymore, but she knows she's stuck with me. We sit around the house and argue over some of the most insignificant shit like we're on *Jerry Springer* or somethin'. For example, she'll say, "Hadjii, I can't believe you forgot today was my birthday. I hate you! I hate you! I'ma leave you and take half of everything you own. I'm takin' half yo shit." And I be like,

"Whateva. Whateva. It ain't mine, bitch. It ain't mine. Half of everythang I own *ain't* mine. BOO-YOW!" But even though I might be lettin' myself go at home, those women at the job think I'm a beautiful muthafucka. And you can use that shit as leverage at home when you feel like ya woman ain't treatin' ya right, like, "What? What'chou mean you ain't talkin' to me? I ain't all that? Oh, well there are several women in the world who beg to differ. Every day a different one of 'em rolls up on me. You don't believe me? Well why you think they built that special ramp goin' up to my office? I rest my case!"

But the craziest thing about a black person in their first real job is that it's the first time you ever deal with Real White People. That's right. Real white people. See, black and white kids can grow up together and play and all that, but those ain't real white people, cause everybody's the same age and basically kids are kids. Then ya get older and ya go to high school and all that and you have a couple of white friends, you get along well with white people, white schoolteachers, whatever, but black people still spend most of their time with other black people and white people spend most of their time with other white people. Nothing racist about it. That's just what happens. You're from a black family that lives in a black neighborhood around other black families and their black kids, and you go to a black church and hang out at the black park or at the black mall, so ya spend most of your time around black people, and again it's the same for whites, Asians, etc. When I got to college I met some brothas from Atlanta who had never had a white kid in their class before. White people freaked them out. Sometimes they'd even come up to me and say, "Damn, folk. I don't see how you deal wit' dem crackers like dat shawty? I ain't used to dat shit. Putcha boy up on game." Then on the other hand I knew this one white girl from some mountain town somewhere who had never been around any black people. She was in a time capsule, still runnin' around callin' people "colored" and shit. I guess the Internet ain't quite gotten to everybody.

Now in places like Atlanta, New York, L.A., D.C., and maybe three other places in America, you can actually walk into an all-black advertising agency or an all-black law firm. I remember the first time I had a meeting with an all-black investment agency, it blew my mind. I walk in and see this nice colorful lobby with the black receptionist, and the black magazines in the waiting area, and all the black business people walking around in suits, and I felt like I was on a UPN sitcom or something. Like, "Damn. This shit actually happens." But that's rare. Matter of fact, it's so rare that whenever people see an all-black business doing well, you know who's the most surprised? Other black people. We don't even believe it. And you can tell, because when a black person sees another black person with their own business doing well we all do the same thing. We get impressed by the dumbest shit. You walk into a white doctor's office, I don't care how nice it is, all you do is sit down and think, "I'm in a doctor's office." We walk into a black doctor's office that looks halfway decent and we lose our fuckin' minds just because the lights are working. "Alright, this is nice. They got business cards and shit. A waitin' area. Music in the background! *Go 'head! Go 'head!* They got *Time* magazine. Ooh! Ooh! Look! They got a sign that says *Doctor's Office.* Y'all doin' the damn thang."

And we're like that because as much as I hate to admit it, we're not used to seeing black people doing well. When I was growin' up it was a big deal whenever you saw a black something. You'd be like, they got a black doctor? Is that a black lawyer? I hope you're in that black teacher's class next year. That school's got a black principal? Black dentist? They got a black quarterback?! A black coach? They done put a nigga in space? Is that a black judge? Pass me those binoculars—oh it's a Haitian. Can we take credit for a Haitian? Cause our parents grew up back in the day, so they didn't get a fair shot at opportunities like we did. So for a black person, having a good job meant you either worked at the hospital, some factory, you were in the military, a teacher, or a preacher. Period. Wait. A couple of people owned their own businesses. Throw them in there. After that, period! And if neither of your parents had one of those jobs, you had a shitty Christmas where you just got "lots of love" every year.

These days race relations are far better than they used to be, at least amongst the young folks, and I really have to give MTV and rap music most of the credit. When I was a kid there were only like five or six black people out.

Eddie Murphy, Michael Jackson, Prince, Stevie Wonder, Lionel Richie, and Mr. T. Oh, and throw Magic Johnson in there. Then rap music came along and after a slow grind in the beginning, BOOM! All of the sudden it blew up. Now I'm damn near surprised when I see white people on MTV, to tell the truth. So times have changed, but before we go off dancin' in the streets, you must remember, those ain't Real White People. I'm talking about the white people ya uncle's been bitchin' about all these years. I'm talking about the ones in the dress shirt and khakis with no socks and loafers with the sleeves rolled up so you can see the Rolex. I'm talkin' about the ones with some power. Da Man. Yep, you went to school, picked a field, and studied hard, so "Da Man will see you now."

Now Da Man has a funny way of letting you know he or she's Da Man. Wait. Lemme set this up right. Attention all white people. I'm about to let'chall in on a little secret. No matter how well you get along with a black person. Y'all could have a great relationship in the office. They could be your best friend from childhood. Y'all can be business partners. Hell, y'all can even get married and have children together. But no matter how well y'all get along, a black person never ever EVER forgets that they are black and you are *white*. Don't take it personal. That's just how we are. Matter of fact an old man once told me a story. Went like this.

"Once upon a time, a long long time ago on a cold and dreary day, there was a man, a black man, walking through the wilderness. And as he was walking through the wilderness he looked down at the ground and noticed a frozen snake laying stiff at his feet. So being the warm and compassionate, positive black man that he was, he kneeled down and picked the snake up and placed the snake in his coat pocket. Ya know, like in one of them inside pockets close to ya bosom? One of them inside pockets close to ya chest? Yeah, he put it in one of those pockets and then continued on his journey.

"Now after the man walked a few miles the snake begin to warm up and thaw out, and it began to wiggle around a little bit. And the soothing skin of the vibrating and lively snake felt good rubbing up against the man's heart. So much so that it even brought a smile to the man's face, for now he had a companion to accompany him as he came closer to his destination, and all the sudden the man didn't seem quite as cold anymore because now the snake was helping to keep him warm. They were helping each other. They were a team. A partnership. They had an understanding, at least so he thought. Then two or three minutes later, the man dropped to his knees and fell face first into the snow, and the snake slowly crawled out of the man's jacket and slithered off on his merry way. The man was dead, Hadjii. Dead to study war no mo'. The moral of the story is, don't'chou let them crackers warm up to ya. Ya can't trust'em! They'll stop ya dead in ya tracks. Now gimme fifty cent."

"Hmm?" I replied. "I'm about to go inside and buy some bubblegum, so I can't give you fifty cents, but that was a very compelling story, Mr. Random Old Black Man

Standing in Front of the Corner Store. I'll never forget it. Anyway, see ya later, Mr. Random Old Black Man Standing in Front of the Corner Store. By the way, try not to steal my bike."

But then again, on the other hand, you've got all these black folks who downright adore and worship white people and believe that "If it ain't white, it ain't right." Black people who use phrases like "You gotta learn how to play the white man's game" and "You gotta get on the inside before you can see the upside." And a bunch of other theories like that. Which, don't get me wrong, I'm an open-minded person so I can see where they're coming from, but on the other hand, I believe that there's no bigger statement that you can make than being yourself. Unless of course "ya self" ain't shit. Then you might need to go copy a nigga or two.

So you grow up with all these thoughts in ya mind. And even if you don't believe it, it's still in your brain, at least you remember ya heard it. It's probably stored in some part of your brain where ya keep the rest of the crazy shit you've heard over the years. Like if ya eat Nerds and drink Coke at the same time, your stomach will explode, and other urban-legend shit like that. So you never forget they're white. It's kind of like how a married man can be coworkers with a happily married woman thirty years his junior, and get along perfectly well with no signs of sexual harassment or nothing, but that woman will never forget that he's still a man. She knows he's sneaking a peek whenever the opportunity presents itself. That's just how people are.

And it's even worse when you're dealing with black people, because black people are very observant. We rely on our instincts a lot, because being black in America is like a twenty-four-hour-a-day job. We don't get caught slippin' too often, cause we can't afford to. For example, if I'm in the bank in July and a dude walks in wearing a trench coat, I get the fuck out the bank. Now maybe I'm paranoid, but I ain't never been shot up in a bank either. See what I'm sayin'?

So no matter how much we may like a white person we're always thinking that there might be a little bit of Da Man lurking inside 'em somewhere, cause just when you think everything's on the up and up and you let your guard down a Confederate flag'll fall out of their pocket or something, and now your feelings are hurt because you let your emotions get involved.

So you're working with Da Man for a few months, and you know how those first few months of a new job are. You're trying to learn your position and feel everybody out while also trying to figure out what corners can be cut and who's the pushover and who's the bitch and stuff like that, and much to my dismay, my boss doesn't seem to have too much of Da Man in 'em. He compliments me on the good job I'm doing and praises me for my work ethic. More time goes by and I sort of become their go-to guy.

"Hadjii, next week's event's really important and I'd feel a lot better if you were in charge of it. I know you'll do a good job." Well, thank you, Mr. Man. By the way, gimme a raise. "Sure thing, Hadjii." Wow. I'm really digging this dude. Mr. Whitey ain't Da Man. He's a great guy. And this makes me feel good, because I've been working hard to do a good job. Because white people, I'm gonna let'chall in on another secret. I mean I'm about to let you in on a secret shared amongst black folks that ranks up there with when the revolution's goin' down and shit like that. Here it is.

Every black person that works around white people, no matter what the setting, feels like they have to represent the entire African American race at all times. Sounds crazy, but trust me, it's true. We'll wake up in the morning with a broken neck, bird flu, and three bullet wounds in our spine, but we will not call in sick. Cause we love our job? No. Cause they need me at work? No. Cause we need the money? Yes, but no. We won't call in because we don't want them thinkin' all niggas don't wanna work. That's right. We cannot let the black community down! We'll speed to work because we don't want them thinkin' niggas gotta be late all the time. I would cuss that dumbass executive out for not giving us Presidents' Day off, but I don't want them thinkin' all niggas love the fuckin' presidents. Empty my trash can. Then they'll be thinkin' all niggas are good for is emptying the trash. Then again, if I don't empty the trash, they'll think all niggas is junky? What's a nigga to do?

So you press onward and eventually all of the staff becomes one big happy family, and ya know what happens when you and all your coworkers become one big happy family? They start getting "comfortable" witcha. And ya know what happens when people start getting comfortable witcha? They wanna spend more time witcha. And ya know what happens when people start wantin' to spend more time witcha? They want you to go to lunch with them. And when you start spending time with people and hanging out with people and going to lunch with 'em, ya know what happens? A lot of dumb shit.

Then they start joking with you more, and the more they joke, the closer they come to crossing the line by saying subliminally offensive shit that you can't quite tell if it's intentional or not. Like they'll come in your office and say:

BOSS: I'm about to go to lunch. Wanna come?
ME: Nah, I'm tryin' to wrap this project up.
BOSS: Oh forget about that. You can finish when you
    get back. Come on. Lunch is on me.

Next thing ya know you're at lunch at some barbecue-buffet joint (because white male supervisors in the South love barbecue), and suddenly you find yourself knee-deep in one of the most awkward conversations you've ever had.

BOSS: Boy I'll tell ya, you people sure can eat.
ME: My people?
BOSS: Yeah. Young guys. When I was young I could
    really put it down. Can't anymore. Damn
    heartburn.

ME: Umm-hmm.

BOSS: So Hadjii, let's talk. Do you know why I hired you?

ME: Cause I was qualified?

BOSS: Yeah that too, but really, I thought the office needed some color, ya know.

ME: What?

BOSS: Yeah, colorful people. Energetic. Lively. Vivacious. You're a personality and I like that.

ME: Umm-hmm.

BOSS: And when I saw that you'd graduated from UGA it was a done deal as far as I was concerned. I love Georgia football. Did you play?

ME: No.

BOSS: That's odd. I figured you were there to play football or basketball or something.

ME: What?

BOSS: Well look at your physique. Most guys your size are pretty athletic. So, got any kids?

ME: Am I supposed to?

BOSS: Guy your age? Sure.

ME: Umm-hmm. Well, I'm goin' up to the bar to get some cantaloupe. You want somethin'?

BOSS: Nah, but make sure you try that watermelon. I'm sure you'll like it.

ME: Huh?

BOSS: It's juicy.

ME: Ya know, Whitey, I don't know what you're up to, but when I figure it out, we're gonna have some problems.

And lunch with white people is always hard because, God knows, you want to order the chicken, but you don't want'em thinkin' all niggas eat chicken. That's right. Grilled salmon again.

But what's even worse is when you have to have lunch with the old white dude in the office. Ya know, like the old white dude who founded the company and he's well respected in the community, so whenever he comes around it's a big deal? That guy. Now this guy doesn't mean any harm. Actually, he's probably a really nice guy who thinks he's just making conversation. The only problem is that he doesn't understand that eighty-five percent of everything he has to say is offensive as hell to the rest of the world.

See, he loves to share his personal stories and experiences with you, and there's nothing wrong with that. It's just that he tends to forget that he grew up during a time when black people had to sit at the back of the bus. So his stories about the good ole days don't always bring that same sense of nostalgia to us, but you've gotta sit there and hear him out anyway.

"Hadjii, I really think you're a good writer for a black guy, and in all honesty I find it amazing that a boy like you can be so articulate. Even though I don't understand half of anything you say, at least you come close. Especially being a colored from the South. Most coloreds from the South tend to just grunt and snort to communicate. So I'm in awe right now. See, back in my day, weren't too many educated coloreds around. Matter of fact, most of the women were slow on the uptake too, but hey, somebody had to have the babies, right? Yet you always had a few people who managed to be somewhat intelligent, even though they weren't white, or male.

"Matter of fact, you remind me of this one fella named Lamont who used to shine my shoes back in 1969. See, Lamont was a multitalented Negro just like you. He could shine shoes, sing songs, dance, and make you a mighty fine cheese sandwich simultaneously. So I gave Lamont an opportunity. I gave him a job as my company's official shoe-shining, cheese-sandwich-making, tap-dancing boy. Well, needless to say, everybody loved him. He was a real card, and took a lot of pride in his work. Lamont could clean an office spick and span so good that you could see your face on your desk top, and not even Frank Sinatra could come close to Lamont's rendition of 'Dixie.' Hell, I used to have'em sing it to me sometimes when it wasn't even my birthday. And every morning when I got to work, I'd take my shoes off and give Lamont my socks so he could get all the lint off 'em, and wouldn't ya know it, two hours later he'd come up to me and say, 'Here's ya socks, sir. As fresh as a baby's bottom.' Then he'd walk away just as happy as he could be.

"So I promoted Lamont and made him head chef in our company's cafeteria. Now I'll admit that he struggled a little at first trying to learn how to cook linguini and other classier entrees, because at the time all Lamont knew how to prepare were soul-food dishes. Ya know, Kool-Aid, pork 'n' beans, bananas, grease, and other black delicacies, but he stuck with it. Just like you're sticking with it. And even though times were rough, good ole Lamont never complained.

"Sometimes Lamont would come into my office and say, 'Thirty-five cents an hour ain't enough to provide for my family, boss.' So I would try to meet Lamont halfway on some things. I'd say, 'Well, I've got an idea for a pay increase. Instead of you spending thirty-five cents a day, which is an hour of your current salary, on bus fare, how about you invest in a sleeping bag and then you can just stay here.' I could tell he liked the idea a lot, because he began to weep. Then Christmas would roll around and Lamont would be upset because he didn't have enough money to get his kids their annual Christmas loaf of bread that they were so eagerly anticipating. So once again, I came to the rescue with yet another brilliant idea. 'Hey Lamont,' I said. 'Know what the problem is? Number one, those kids don't need an entire loaf of bread. Just give'em all one slice and let'em play with that. And number two, you're trying to raise a family on only one income. Here's what I'll do. I'll give you an extra seven dollars a month, if you let me sleep with your wife once a week.' Once again, Lamont began to weep and I could tell he was thankful that I had so unselfishly gone out of my way to provide. See, I didn't have to do that, but there are certain people ya just want to make it in life, and Lamont was one of those people. Just like you.

"So Hadjii, I guess the million-dollar question is, Are you married? And if so, how does your wife look?"

My Mama
Can Read This Part

So there you have it. From my childhood to adulthood, from school to church to work, from The Boogie Man to The White Man, Act One of this production is over, so you can all breathe easy now. This wasn't the tell-all autobiography that you were afraid of. No dark secrets to reveal, no pain to dwell on, and no revenge to seek.

So to the boss who told me, "Henry, you might as well get used to it because you'll be cleaning toilets for the rest of your life," you're home free. I let you off the hook.

To the guidance counselor who said, "You'll never make it at the University of Georgia," I'm not going to hold your stupidity against you. And to everyone who said I'd never make it as a writer, it's not your fault, because obviously you'll never make it as a psychic. And to everybody who was worried about me exposing them, or sharing our personal and intimate moments, conversations, or whatever, trust me, I'm still your boy. Your marriages, jobs, and images are safe. Chivalry, loyalty, respect, and honor still exist.

Because I could've talked about racism, betrayal, heartache, failure, and all the other things that make you go *ooooh*. Or the parties, the sex, and all those things that make you go *ahhhh*. But my parents, my family, and all of the others around me did the best they could to make me see that there was more to life than that. So it isn't even worth mentioning. Therefore, I'd rather talk about dirty underwear instead.

Hope you enjoyed,
Hadjii

P.S. For those of you who would like to know more about my sex life, partying, and my experiences with betrayal, racism, criminal activity, and heartache: Don't worry. It's coming. I just had to save some shit for the second book.

Just kiddin', Mama,
Hadjii

Thank You

To God and everyone who has made my life easier, without your support, prayers, and generosity this truly wouldn't be possible. There are too many of you to name, so I won't even try for fear of leaving someone out, but you all know who you are. Both past and present. Thanks for everything.

About the Author

Henry Cameron Hand was born and raised in Brunswick, Georgia. Hadjii is a nickname that was given to him by his father when he was a toddler. To most of the world's surprise, Hadjii actually grew up in a trailer park, but the black neighborhoods were only a two-minute bicycle ride away, if that makes you feel any better. Often Hadjii would spend his childhood summers in either Jacksonville, Florida, or Atlanta, Georgia, depending on which aunt was brave enough to take him in for three months.

Hadjii wrote, directed, and starred in his first film, *Somebodies*, which had its premiere at the Sundance Film Festival in 2006. A television series based on *Somebodies*, also written by, directed by, starring, and executive-produced by Hadjii, is slated to appear on BET, the first original sitcom ever to appear on that network. *Don't Let My Mama Read This: A Southern-Fried Memoir* is his first book.